Drumming

Ancient Wisdom for Unleashing the Human Spirit and Building Community

To: Rose
Hedzoleh (peace)!
6/4/16

Kokomon Clottey

With Foreword and Contributions by Dennis "Den" Hill, M.D.

Editor: Nancy Grimley Carleton
Artistic renderings of symbols: Dennis Hill, M.D.
Cover design and book composition: Jennifer Geib
Back cover photograph: John Veltri
Transcriptions of rhythms: Matthew Hill
Pencil sketches of drums: Amana Harris

Sankofa Publishing
P.O. Box 23503
Oakland, CA 94623 USA
T: (510) 652-7901
F: (510) 652-8233
Website: www.ancestralhealing.com

If you are unable to find this book in your local bookstore, you may order it from the publisher. Quantity discounts for organizations are available.

First Printing Spring 2004

Library of Congress Cataloging-in-Publication Data

Clottey, Kokomon 1949 -
      Mindful Drumming: Ancient Wisdom for Unleasing the Human Spirit
      and Building Community
      p. 180

Includes: index
1. Spirituality - 2. Community relations - 3. Drumming - 4. African people

ISBN: 0-9719678-0-6

Dedication

This book is dedicated to
the millions of voiceless children of the world,
who, in our darkest hour,
caught in the abyss of fear,
are the hope of tomorrow.

Make no mistake:
Love is larger than fear.
It is naive to believe otherwise.
If in doubt, ask God!

Make no mistake:
Tomorrow will come.
Yes! Spring will come
after the dark, chilling cold.

God's challenge to you is this:
No child should ever live in fear.
No child should ever be homeless.
No child should ever be visited by hunger.

Let the children play!
Let the children laugh!
Let the children dance!
Let the children sing!

And may all children be happy!

~ Kokomon Clottey

Contents

List of Exercises

Practices to Unleash the Human Spirit

Key to the Symbols

The symbols on the cover and on the opening page of each of the seven primary chapters are artistic renderings by Dr. Den Hill of ancient Adinkra symbols from the Akan tribe of Ghana, West Africa. Their general meanings are listed below.

Cover: ***Gye nyame*** Except God

Chapter One: ***Sankofa*** Go back to fetch it

Chapter Two: ***Dwennimmen*** Humility and strength

Chapter Three: ***Sunsum*** Spirituality

Chapter Four: ***Nyame nwu na mawu*** Perpetual Existence

Chapter Five: ***Dono*** Rhythm

Chapter Six: ***Funtummireku-Denkyemmireku*** Unity in Diversity

Chapter Seven: ***Gye nyame*** Except God

Foreword

Earth People

As each group seeks its separate
Roots and origins,
Society fractures along a thousand fissure lines.
When neighbors distance themselves
From neighbors, continue your
Uncompromising quest
For your true roots.
In the deepest regions of your lives,
Seek out the primordial roots of humankind.
Then you will without fail discover
The stately expanse of spirit
unfolding in the depths of your lives.
Here is the home, the dwelling place,
To which humankind traces its original existence.
Beyond all borders,
Beyond all differences of gender and race,
Here is a world offering true proof
of our humanity.
If one reaches back to these fundamental roots,
All become friends and comrades.
To realize this is to emerge from
The earth.

~ Daisaku Ikeda

This excerpt from a much longer 1993 poem inspired me to "seek out the primordial roots of humankind." The author, Japanese Buddhist philosopher and writer Daisaku Ikeda, wrote this poem following the civil unrest in Watts in 1992. Ikeda predicted that the new age will be led by the continent of Africa, the home of the original people.

My search for primordial roots would indeed lead me to Africa, initially in the form of a year-long mentorship training program with teachers from the Dagara tribe in West Africa who were living in Oakland at the time, and later through my association with the author of this book, Kokomon Clottey.

I first met Kokomon on a beautiful summer day in 1999. I was participating in a community event in Oakland to welcome and rename the *Artship*. This ship had served as former troop transport vessel named the *Golden Bear* after being built as an art deco passenger ship commissioned during World War II. It was donated to the City of Oakland to be restored and remodeled as a floating Art and Culture Center and the U.S. headquarters of the International Peace University. Oakland Mayor Jerry Brown and Nobel Prize winner Wole Soyinka of Nigeria, one of the foremost writers in Africa today, were on hand to help with the dedication.

A large crowd had gathered for the event at Oakland's Estuary Park. The sun was shining brightly, the mood was festive, and the decorations were colorful. Suddenly, a large sound boomed across the park, grabbing everyone's attention. The punctuated drum sounds soon settled into an infectious primal rhythm. People began to move as if pulled by an invisible force. As the eyes of the crowd focused on the stage, we all were struck by the beaming presence of a large African man dressed in bright traditional attire. Although he was but a solitary drummer, everyone seemed to be gathered in by his playing. I was fascinated by the positive influence of the lone drum on me and the people around me. I was determined to meet the drummer.

The drummer's name turned out to be Kokomon Clottey, a medicine man (or shaman) from the Ga tribe in Ghana, West Africa, who currently runs the Attitudinal Healing Connection in West Oakland, California. Kokomon is a gentle, warm, and powerful man of great spiritual wisdom. Since our initial meeting, I have attended a number of his workshops and events and have benefited greatly from his guidance. We have developed a warm and abiding friendship which continues to this day.

My quest to discover and understand the primordial roots of

humankind had led me to Kokomon; soon it would lead me to Africa itself. In the summer of 2000, I had the good fortunate to travel with Kokomon and his American-born wife, Aeeshah, on their first annual cultural tour to Ghana.

As we boarded the jet for the seventeen-hour-long journey, Kokomon asked those of us traveling with him to remove our wrist-watches. He had already told us not to bring laptop computers or cell phones, so that we could immerse ourselves in the local culture. I could understand not bringing a computer or a phone, but how could we tell time without our watches?

After we had settled into our accommodations at a small hotel near a local Ga village, the answer to that question became clear.

Each morning before sunrise, small birds, such as humming-birds and finches, would begin to sing. As each morning progressed, larger birds, such as doves and sparrows, would join in, and finally the largest birds, such as crows, would enter into the joyous symphony of sound. Kokomon told us that with this musical celebration it is as if the birds are saying, "Here comes the king, the morning sun!"

In the evening, this process would repeat itself in reverse. Just before sunset, the birds would sing in what sounded like gratitude to the sun for being there all day. This progressive symphony happened "like clockwork" each morning and evening. Signals like this, along with our newly awakened attention to the position of the sun in the sky, let us know the time in a natural way. I never once missed my watch!

Kokomon's people, the Ga-Adagbe tribe of Ghana, West Africa, are traditional villagers who fish and farm for their livelihood, just as they have done for centuries. Each morning before sunrise, the villagers are up and about, beginning their daily tasks. I could hear the rhythmic shuffling of their feet along the dirt road outside my window, along with the rhythm of the distant ocean waves and the singing birds. When I looked out, I could see the villagers chewing on what I later learned was a local root they called *taakotsa* (pronounced *ta-ko-cha*). They chew *taakotsa* in meditative silence as they go about their morning routine, cleaning their teeth and exercising

their jaws in this ancient, natural way.

The Ga people live with the sunrise and sunset, the ocean tides, and the other rhythms of the natural world. Their daily tasks, such as pulling in the fishing nets and planting new crops, are all done with a collective, rhythmic effort. These village people live communally in every respect. They treasure their children and their elders, and they honor their departed ancestors. Each individual is considered to be a spirit in human form, and each individual is treated as an invaluable part of the community. The traditional drum is a central and essential element of their culture.

As a Westerner, I was struck that even in the bustling urban environment of the capital city of Accra, the people cooperated with one another. I observed that even on the crowded highway leading into the city, which is jammed with a panoply of trucks, automobiles, and pedestrians, everything seemed to move in rhythmic way, forming a kind of elegant dance of people and machines.

Everywhere we went in Ghana, people looked us directly in the eye. No one ignored us; our presence, however brief, was always acknowledged. How different from the often anonymous, alienated, and alienating experience of walking through our city streets in America, or riding on our public transit!

In our modern, mechanized, Westernized world, we seem to be constantly under time pressure. We have to keep checking our watches to stay on schedule, and we don't seem to have much time for our closest friends and loved ones, let alone time to acknowledge the presence of strangers we encounter in passing.

Most of us commute some distance through traffic or hectic transit systems to get to our workplaces, which are generally far removed from where we live. Rather than moving together cooperatively and in rhythm, we often seem to be competing with one another, whether in traffic, at work, or even in play. Because of this, we often feel isolated, alienated, and alone. And our urban highways, buildings, sidewalks, and often sterile landscaping tend to keep us divorced from the rhythms of the natural world as well as separated from one another.

No wonder we need to turn elsewhere in our search for the

timeless and primordial roots of our true humanity. From the time-less African Ga culture, Kokomon—medicine man, musician, and author—brings an important healing teaching to our modern world. He calls the method he teaches *mindful drumming meditation*, and it is based on the fundamentals of his communal Ga culture. Through mindful drumming, we can get in touch with our deeper self and thereby feel connected with the humanity of other people as well. The benefits of mindful drumming include empowerment, the cultivation of deep listening, a chance to tap the higher power within, community building, inner peace, deep happiness, and heightened self-esteem.

I have experienced all of these benefits firsthand, both in my journey to Ghana, Africa, and through my participation in community drumming circles with Kokomon and others back in the United States. The Western world hungers and thirsts for these very benefits. As a physician interested in health and the healing arts, I consider it my great honor to commend to you Kokomon's culturally based therapy of mindful drumming meditation as presented in his book, *Mindful Drumming: Ancient Wisdom for Unleashing the Human Spirit and Building Community,* which you hold in your hands.

~Den Hill, M.D.
Oakland, California

Preface

Drum!
If your heart beats,
Drum!
For the breath of life,
Drum!
For those yet to be born,
Drum!
For happiness,
Drum!
For world peace,
Drum!

~ Kokomon Clottey

How serendipitous for you to be holding this book in your hands! In the culture where I was born, there are no accidents. Everything is seen as part of the divine order. Therefore, it is no accident that you have come across this book. My hope is that it will guide you to a deeper unfolding of your spirit, unleashing the power that lies within you as you connect with the community around you.

Whatever the case may be, in the words of my people I say, *Oyiwaladon* (pronounced *o-yee-wah-lah-don*), which in English means both "May eternal blessing and grace be bestowed upon you" and "Thank you!"

I hope and trust that this book, *Mindful Drumming: Ancient Wisdom for Unleashing the Human Spirit and Building Community,* has arrived in your life at the right time, especially considering the erosion of trust and the sense of insecurity in the modern world. We search perpetually for happiness, which my people call *mishe,* but all too often end up living in a state of perpetual fear. We human

beings need grace and help from the Great Spirit, or *Nyogboh*, the kind of help that will assist us in being joyful, peaceful, and happy. Practicing the easy and fun exercises in this book will help you open to the grace and help from the Great Spirit and find the true path to joy, peace, and happiness.

As a little boy growing up among the Ga-Adagbe people of Ghana, West Africa, I saw and experienced many rituals and ancient ceremonies where drumming was one of the most basic features. I found this drumming potent and mesmerizing, especially when the dancers who followed the rhythm and vibration of the drum entered into deep trance, an altered state of consciousness powerful to behold.

From my childhood on, I embarked on a lifelong quest to understand the multiple states of consciousness that are available to all of us. I was particularly interested in investigating and then sharing what I learned about the wisdom of the indigenous culture I was born into, and I was eventually initiated as a master drummer and medicine man by my elders.

My journey has blessed me with many opportunities and many teachers and guides who deepened my understanding along the way. I met one of my early teachers when I was thirteen—my god-father Kofi Ghanaba, an African mystic, journalist, and musician, whose inspiration and wisdom opened me to my own mystical path. What I love most about the wisdom I received from Ghanaba is the great breadth of his knowledge and a kind of emotional literacy which arose from his deep connection to sound and rhythm.

Over time, I have come to see that our separation from *Nyogboh*, the Great Spirit, lies at the root of the dysfunction and breakdown of numerous families and the communities in the United States of America, where I have been fortunate to have lived since immigrating here as a young man in 1977.

By calling this book *Mindful Drumming: Ancient Wisdom for Unleashing the Human Spirit and Building Community,* I hope to suggest that although our spirits—and our communities—may be entrapped, they can be unleashed. Mindful drumming provides a natural, effective, and fun process for liberating us and removing the blocks to our wholeness. Through a direct experience of the twin realities of rhythm and vibration, we can be transported into a state of *mishe,* or happiness.

By following the path outlined in this book, you will discover that there is an ocean of untapped innate wisdom that the Western world has largely ignored. You may experience a reawakening of simple truths you knew as a child but which were ridiculed into nothingness or simply forgotten. This book will teach you how to unleash the strength of your spirit and come into your full power as a human being as you learn to be mindful of rhythm, vibration, and sound. You will learn the simple methods of *mindful drumming meditation,* which is as easy as learning to pay attention to the rhythm of your own footsteps. Yes, your very own footsteps!

This book is for people who are serious about enhancing their ability to be in touch with their authentic power. Through unleashing the spirit, we are better able to create positive relationships that are deep, strong, pure, and whole. When our spirit is unleashed, the gate of heaven opens with its infinite possibilities. Love, peace, and happiness—the essence of our being—become palpable. When a person is feeling this *mishe* (happiness), everyone takes notice. Such a person walks like an African lion, with supreme confidence, exuding an aura of authenticity, power, compassion, affection, and a deep sense of intuition.

Opening this book demonstrates your deep desire to reconnect with *Nyogboh*—the Great Spirit—with your ancestors, and with yourself. *Akwaba!* Welcome! The path of mindful drumming awaits you, and through its grace your deepest desires will be fulfilled. *Nyogboh* is always present, eagerly awaiting our return with open arms.

~Kokomon Clottey
West Oakland, California

Acknowledgments

What I know about music,
cannot fill a thimble,
but what I feel about it,
can fill a barrel.
The secret to peace of mind,
as I have found,
is to live and love abundantly. . . .
Love as abundantly as you
ever possibly can . . .
and you will find peace.

~ Kofi Ghanaba

It would be naive and arrogant for me to think that I came up with all of the information in this book on my own. I am aware that this information came *through* me, from *Atta-Naa-Nyogboh*, Father-Mother-God, as revealed by thousands of generations of my ancestors. I am humble knowing that I am standing on their shoulders and telling you all that I see, hear, smell, and feel. I am very grateful for this enormous gift, which I graciously accept.

In addition, I have received assistance from many of my fellow humans, companions on this journey of spirit. In Africa, I benefited from the wisdom not only of the members of my community but most particularly of my godfather, Kofi Ghanaba, a great shaman and the only African musician ever to have been inducted into the Hall of Fame for jazz. Other wisdom bearers from my motherland to whom I am indebted are Bro Ishmael Tetteh, the founder of the Etherean Mission in Accra, Ghana, West Africa, and Brother Mustafeh Tetteh, founder of the African Arts and Music Academy also in Accra. I am grateful for the inspiration of Professor C. K. Ladzekpo, originally from Ghana, who is currently a faculty member at the University of California at Berkeley as well as founder and director of the African Dance Ensemble.

I have also been inspired by many different spiritual teachers during my time in the United States. These teachers include Dr. William Honaday of the Science of Mind Church in Los Angeles and the Reverend Andrew DaPassano of the Temple of Esoteric Science, also in Los Angeles. I was also deeply touched by Dr. Gerald (Jerry) Jampolsky, the developer of the principles of attitudinal healing and one of the most important thinkers of our time. His book *Love Is Letting Go of Fear* integrates spiritual wisdom, psychology, and social theory. I am blessed to have known him personally and to have adopted him as my surrogate father upon the death of my biological father in 1995.

The Reverend Matthew Fox, a modern-day saint and fearless voice, validated my spiritual path with his extraordinary book *Original Blessing*. He has inspired me with his passionate desire for justice and his openness to learning the wisdom of the indigenous mind. I have been his student and friend since we met at the Windstar Conference in Aspen, Colorado, in 1995. At the Naropa-University of Creation Spirituality founded by Dr. Fox in Oakland, students can even acquire a Master's degree in indigenous wisdom. I am deeply grateful to the late singer John Denver, a true seeker, and to Howard Thurman, John Robbins, Marianne Williamson, Dr. Diane Cirincione, and Dr. Michael Beckwith. All of them are spiritual warriors and teachers who have inspired me and my work.

I also wish to acknowledge the helpful suggestions and insights I received from Dr. Douglas Ziedonis at the Robert Wood Johnson Medical School in New Jersey. I appreciate his friendship and his wisdom in helping me to actually test the mindful drumming approach with his patients and community building efforts. His large federal research grant funded by the Center for Substance Abuse Treatment (CSAT) provided the opportunity to bridge ancient wisdom with current research technique. In addition, I am grateful for the abundant encouragement, support, and inspiration of Bob Heinrichs.

My sincere gratitude to Jennifer Geib for reading the first draft and making important suggestions, and for all her unfettered support in designing the front, back cover and book layout. Many thanks as well go to John Veltri for the photograph used on the back cover, and to Matthew Hill for his transcriptions of traditional African rhythms and mindful drumming rhythms, which are presented in Appendix C. Amana Harris for the drum sketches and Ralph Chapuis for reading the manuscript and making corrections.

I am very grateful and appreciative for the guidance I have received from my editor, Nancy Grimley Carleton, and from Dr. Dennis "Den" Hill, who wrote the Foreword and contributed throughout the book. They both made significant contributions to the shaping and careful editing of the manuscript over the course of two years, and I am greatly in debt to them. I claim them as my friends, my family, and my allies.

Finally, my deepest appreciation and thanks to my companion on this life path, my wife and partner in work, Aeeshah Ababio-Clottey. *Oyiwaladon!* Thank you!

~Kokomon Clottey

Introduction

There are many ways leading to God;
I have chosen that of music and dance.

~ Rumi

The Power of Mindful Drumming

At our center in West Oakland called the Attitudinal Healing Connection, my wife, Aeeshah, and I facilitate Racial Healing Circles. In these circles, participants share some of the deepest and most painful aspects of the racism and racial fears engendered in the American culture. In order to create a safe container for this sharing, we always start our Racial Healing Circles with thirty minutes of drumming together, all following a simple series of rhythms. We do this to build community and to reconnect everyone to our ancestors, allowing us to transform the ancient pain of mistrust and misunderstanding into hope and love so that we can more fully express our beauty and goodness as human beings.

The participants in our Racial Healing Circles have confirmed that by drumming together first, they come to experience a sense of deep connection with the other members of the circle even before the verbal interactions begin. Out of this sense of connection and community, they report that they are able to share deeply intimate experiences with the other people in the circle, even those they may have initially mistrusted out of preexisting judgments, or a fear of being judged. Through the circle of unity created by the power of drumming mindfully together, they can explore their deepest wounding around the highly charged issue of racial relations with others from different backgrounds. This is a profoundly healing experience. Here Aeeshah shares her experience of the power of mindful drumming in this context.

My Experience with Mindful Drumming:
Words from Aeeshah Ababio-Clottey

Kokomon and I began offering our weekly Racial Healing Circles in 1990. We wanted to create a safe place where people from all walks of life and diverse ethnic and racial groups could come together to heal and share their race biographies. The "R" word had been taboo too long in our supposedly advanced society. We knew that it was time for Americans to heal their racial and ethnic wounds. However, we didn't anticipate how difficult it would be or how long we would be holding these dialogues. Let me tell you, they were painful, and people had a tough time opening up! Sometimes there were outbursts, and the group would shut down verbally and emotionally. Our hope was to create a fulfilling experience where diverse people could come together to commune and share with one another authentically. We had group guidelines we read at the beginning of each gathering, and we took a lot of time to establish the agreements that the group would adhere to so that people would feel safe. Even though we had the guidelines and the agreements to support the safety of the group, it was still emotionally and psychologically messy and painful. It would take many sessions before the group would begin to feel like a community.

After about four years of meeting and sharing, we wondered how long we would last! Deepening the conversation about race was painful and complicated. At the close of 1994, Kokomon suggested that we infuse some ancient ways into the Racial Healing Circles. As an experiment, we decided to try a thirty-minute drumming meditation before giving the guidelines for the group. Our very first experience with this validated the power of the drum and the benefits of nonverbal communication. As we drummed, a strong sense of kinship developed in just thirty minutes! We then read the group guidelines, and the deep sense of community was palpable. The depth and quality of the conversation was clearly enhanced. Instead of the usual difficulty and discomfort, participants sharing their race bios were more open and were ready to speak from the heart. They were more willing to talk about the knee-jerk reactions they sometimes experienced in racial and ethnic matters. The drum had deepened the conversation, led to true communing, and validated the connectedness of our humanity. From then on, we always began our Racial Healing Circles with a mindful drumming meditation.

Shortly after this, Kokomon decided to start a mindful drumming meditation circle for world peace and personal healing. I agreed to participate as a way to support him, not particularly expecting that I would receive much from being a participant. These gatherings were different from most of the support groups we led at our center in that there was no dialogue during the meditation—only mindful drumming. However, we would talk at the end of the meditation to share our experiences.

I discovered immediately that mindful drumming provided a shortcut to quieting the mind. Usually in a support group, I would be aware of my preoccupation with judgment, which mostly manifested as noise and confusion in my mind over wanting to let go of judgments and at the same time feeling confronted by them. Even more challenging were my attachments to my perceptions of myself and what others would or would not say. However, during the drumming meditation, I found I could easily and effortlessly stay in the present, letting go of judgments and perceptions of fear and separation without taking note of how the letting go process happened. I would be transported to an inner place of relaxation, joy, and peace. I think the most powerful experience for me was the immediate creation of community and a feeling of happiness.

Being a helper by profession, I usually had a sense of uneasiness in a new group, and a desire to make everyone feel better. This tended to make me feel fear, in that I wanted to change someone or something. However, when we drummed together, I noted that my sense of needing to help would disappear without my even thinking about it. All I heard was the combined heartbeat of the group, and nothing else mattered. We would be drumming, listening, and looking at one another, and a deep sense of peace would come over me like a cool breeze on a hot summer day. I would look at each participant with a deep feeling of love and warmth, as if each person in the group were my very best friend.

Drumming together was powerful and beautiful. Sometimes the

rhythms and sounds of the drum would bring a complete sense of unspeakable serenity that magnified our innate connections, and communion happened almost immediately among the participants. This sense of inner peace stayed with me for long periods of time. The drumming energized my work week and seemed to help me accomplish the work that was my livelihood as well as my service work for the community without burnout and the stress of feeling I was doing too much. The mindful drumming meditation in a group setting helped me to realize the value of having only one goal, which is to experience peace of mind. I stopped thinking about how I was doing several jobs, working full-time in mental health as an assistant program director, volunteering at the Attitudinal Healing Connection, Inc., speaking nationally and internationally, and serving as a trustee of several very important national not-for-profit organizations in addition to being a wife, mother, and grandmother. Instead, I began to see that I was really doing only one job: working on my own heart and mind, letting go of fear and experiencing love in my heart.

After a few sessions, it became very clear to me that I was coming to the drumming circles not to support Kokomon, but for my own joy and personal healing.

In workshops around the country, I have led many different groups in the practice of *mindful drumming meditation,* in which I, as the leader, set a simple rhythm which the others follow. During the course of the meditation, I lead the group through multiple rhythms, each lasting at least three minutes. Following half an hour or an hour or more of drumming together with full conscious awareness, people who started out as strangers leave as friends. In our regular community drumming circles at our Attitudinal Healing Connection center in West Oakland, participants testify to the deep levels of healing and joy they experience. These repercussions carry over into meaningful changes in their day-to-day lives.

When a group of people gather together and create patterns of rhythm and sound on their drums, after a period of time they enter into a state of unity. This state of unity brings with it a deeply profound state of happiness, or *mishe* in the language of my Ga people. Drumming, then, opens the door to *mishe* in action, to happiness in community. The alchemy of communication created by this experience of *mishe* carries with it the seeds of transformation not only for the individual but for all of society.

I have come to understand a number of meanings for the word *communication*. According to *Webster's Dictionary,* the root of the word *communication* comes from the Latin *communis,* meaning "common," which is also the root of the word *community*, and can be defined as "belonging equally to or shared by all." This is the matrix of communication and community upon which mindful drumming is built.

This book presents a theory and practice of individual and community healing through rhythm and sound from an African medicine man's point of view. To aid the Western reader, I have invited my friend and brother Den Hill, an American doctor of medicine who has long traveled a spiritual path and who graciously wrote the Foreword to this book, to share some of his experiences with you; these additions will be inserted from time to time in the text.

Through Western Eyes: Words from Dr. Dennis Hill

I have benefited greatly from attending Kokomon's mindful drumming circles. During these meditations, there is no talking and no leaving the circle once the drumming has begun, so the rhythmic space is not interrupted.

Prior to the drumming, Kokomon instructs everyone about "deep listening" and asks us to watch his hands closely, as well as the hands of others in the drumming circle, so that everyone is following the same rhythmic pattern. As the central figure, Kokomon sets the rhythm, switching to other simple rhythms at intervals to keep everyone alert and in synch with all the others. This reinforces individual feelings of inclusion, which is healthy and empowering.

As Kokomon reminds us at the beginning, we are not there to show off what great drummers we are, or to compete with the other drummers. Our collective intention is to make rhythm together, in unison. This is the key element of community building, finding that common place and building on it.

At the completion of the drumming session, which can last anywhere from thirty minutes to an hour or more, Kokomon asks the

participants to share their experience of drumming with the group. These reports are nearly always positive and often humorous, and the experiences are generally shared in common by many of the participants.

The true value of mindful drumming meditation is not easy to explain in words. It must be experienced by the individual. Nevertheless, having had the opportunity to attend a number of these session, I have uniformly benefited from the experience.

On one early occasion, I was in a drumming circle with approximately twenty-five other people, most of them strangers to me. It was a Friday evening, and many of us had just finished a long day at work, and had to push through the heavy Bay Area traffic just to get to the gathering. Kokomon began the drumming with a simple rhythm, but after a few minutes had gone by, I noticed that the tempo, which had started out slowly had soon sped up. My impression was that we were collectively carrying our impulsive workday rushing into the drumming circle.

But Kokomon, being a master drummer, subtly changed the beat to get us into a more mellow rhythmic space. After a short while, we fell into a synchronized pattern, and I could feel myself beginning to let go a little. I began to be more aware of the people sitting around the circle. I was struck by the unison of the collective hands in motion and the rhythmic space we were creating together. We were truly communing with one another!

As we went farther along this drum journey together, I began to hear a soft singing voice accompanying the drumming. It sounded like a woman's voice, gentle and soothing, like a mother's lullaby. I decided to look up and see who was singing, but when I did, I saw that everyone was drumming. No one in the circle was singing at all! But I continued to hear the melodious voice very clearly. This was an experience that I found very mysterious, but at the end of the session, when it was time to share our individual experiences with the group, I felt safe enough to describe it.

Being a rather private person, I found it amazing that I could talk about such a thing to complete strangers. Although most of us hadn't known each other before the session, it did not feel as if we were strangers at the end. On the contrary, I felt a deep sense of kinship with everyone present. It felt as if I were recounting a dream to family members. It was that easy. On top of that, other people had had similar experiences. There were comments such as "I felt connected to everyone in the circle," and "I heard singing voices, happy voices," "I heard sounds of nature," and so on. Everyone's experience was treated as completely valid. It was quite refreshing, and certainly not an ordinary, everyday experience with other people.

As we said our good-byes at the end of the evening, I felt a much deeper connection to all present, and I experienced a calmer self compared to when I had arrived. I carried that connected, calmer feeling with me even after I left the building and went on my way. Judging by the way people lingered and talked with one another after the session, I'm certain I was not alone in that feeling.

The Transmission of Shamanic Wisdom

You will learn in this book about the secret wisdom and awe-some power of drumming. This wisdom has been safeguarded and transmitted over the centuries by the tribal shaman or medicine man/medicine woman. According to the culture of my birth, and that of many indigenous peoples around the world, a medicine man/medicine woman, or shaman, is a person with occult knowledge, knowledge that originates beyond this world. My people call such persons *tsofa-tse* (pronounced *cho-fa-cheh*), which means a fetish priest or priestess.

For the purposes of this Introduction, let me say that my concern is to interpret the spiritual, or shamanic, codes for healing relative to the tools of rhythm and sound. These codes and tools are gifts bestowed on me by the ancestors, and I have received permission to share them at this point in time. I say "at this point in time," because prior to my journey to the United States of America in 1977, my elders gave me this information but told me I would only be allowed to facilitate the transmission of this wisdom to others "in the fullness of time." I was very young back then, and my elders had impressed upon me the dangers of the reckless application of such awesome powers; that is, if I didn't explain to people how to use the information appropriately, someone could get hurt on an emotional level.

Now, twenty-five years later, through gathering the fruits of my personal journey and through my sharing in group settings, the fullness of time has arrived when I may share the wisdom and knowledge I gleaned from my elders and ancestors with a wider audience through the medium of this book.

From the medicine man point of view, I will present rhythm and sound as a spiritual practice that is mindful, playful, and community-oriented. My focus as a medicine man is to alleviate individual disconnection from spirit, cast light on dysfunctional family issues, and heal unhealthy community experiences.

As you can see, this is not about getting a drum and "beating" on it in a mindless fashion just to "make noise." Nor is it about getting together with a group of people and "jamming" with many different rhythms and individual improvisations. While "making noise" and "jamming" with a drum have their place and can be fun and enlivening, that kind of drumming is not what this book is about.

Rather, the details I am choosing to present are governed by innate, ancestral spiritual wisdom to enhance the understanding of rhythm and sound as central mediums of healing for individuals, families, and communities. *Mindful drumming,* then, is a very specific form of drumming for the purposes of individual and community healing. Mindful drumming, in its most basic sense, involves rhythm and vibration (or sound) practiced in a conscious way whether or not a specific instrument known as a *drum* is involved.

Putting Mindful Drumming into Practice

This book includes specific instructions for readers about drumming and about unleashing the human spirit. In each chapter, I've included at least one exercise, or practice, to help you engage with the principles I am describing. Please take the time to engage in these practices! They allow you to take the material from the written page and translate it into direct experience. All of these exercises are designed to be simple, clear, and fun. With these exercises, you can practice on your own without attending one of my workshops.

You don't even need to have a drum! Of course I hope you'll be inspired enough by the awesome powers of mindful drumming to seek out your very own instrument if you don't already have one (see Appendix B for information on where to get a drum). But in the meantime you can start to get a sense of the power of rhythm and vibration mindfully applied by using your hands on your thighs to tap out the rhythms, or by using a table top or other resonant object. You can do this in the privacy of your own home, although later you might want to invite a friend, or two or three (or more!), to join you in creating a mindful drumming circle, as I'll describe in Chapter Six.

For now, read through the first exercise, set the book aside, and begin the experience!

PRACTICE TO UNLEASH THE HUMAN SPIRIT
EXPERIENCING THE BASICS OF MINDFUL DRUMMING

1. First, turn off your radio, TV, cell phone, beeper, and any other potential source of distraction. Get out your drum, or if you don't have a drum, imagine your thighs to be a drum, or perhaps use your kitchen table. Sit quietly in a comfortable position.

2. Gently tap out three even counts on your drum (or thighs) with the palms of both hands — one, two, three — and then, for the fourth beat, clap your hands.

3. Repeat this simple rhythm of three taps followed by a clap while maintaining equal measurement between counts, using a slow or moderate speed. Continue this pattern at least ten times.

4. Next, experiment with keeping this simple rhythm going for a minimum of three minutes, or longer when you have the time.

See how easy it is? If you stick with it, this simple rhythmic pulse will eventually create a circular motion that can transport you into a trance. A trance is an altered state of consciousness, an abstraction of the mind, a condition that can evoke *mishe*, or happiness. This state provides a gateway to the ancestral, or spirit, world. While you're in this state, you'll be open to intuitive insight, and you may begin to sense subtle sounds, images, or visions that are messages from the realm of spirit.

Tapping out a variety of simple repetitive rhythms while maintaining a meditative state of attention is the essence of mindful drumming. In addition to tapping out rhythms on your drum or on your thighs, you can use movement to experience this rhythmic phenomenon, as I'll be describing in a later chapter.

For now, return to the basic practice in the Introduction any time you want to tap into the essential rhythms evoked in mindful drumming meditation. By allowing yourself to fully experience this rhythm, you'll soon be noticing the rhythms that surround you all the time in daily life—from the rhythm of your footsteps as you walk to the rhythms of your own breath rising and falling with each inhalation and exhalation. And you'll begin to be more aware of the rhythms of the natural world around you, and maybe even see that children in your neighborhood are demonstrating the dynamics of the drumming exercise you just experienced when they jump rope or sing songs in the rhythm of modern-day rap music.

Untapping the power of these essential rhythms to transform your life and unleash the human spirit is as simple as beginning to pay attention!

Chapter One

The Way of Mindful Drumming

Hedzoleh!
Peace!
The courage to choose peace
is an awesome one,
for peace is an orientation of the soul.
In the darkest hour,
when passion takes over reason,
remember that peace is an attribute of love,
not the mere absence of war.
Peace, in a deep sense,
is the ocean
where beauty comes from,
and from where beauty is born.
Kindness,
the true meaning of beauty,
is never without laughter.

~ Kokomon Clottey

The Indigenous Roots of Drumming

Drumming is an ancient indigenous technology that uses the twin realities of rhythm and sound (or vibration) to bring about an alignment of body, mind, and spirit. It offers a natural medium for restoring health and wholeness.

Drumming is also a cross-cultural phenomenon. All indigenous cultures use some sort of drumming in ritual ceremonies. They create synchronistic, harmonic rhythms as tools to get out of the body, to be unbound, to be free to fly like eagles—that is, to experience an altered state of consciousness conducive to happiness and inner peace.

Although in this book I will be sharing the ancestral, timeless wisdom of the Ga people of Ghana, West Africa, I would like to acknowledge that I have encountered similar healing methods used by indigenous cultures the world round, including the indigenous peoples of Papua New Guinea, the Aborigines of Australia, the Pachamama of Ecuador in South America, and the Navaho, Lakota, Hopi, and Apache in North America, to name but a few. This knowledge is universal and perennial, and is not unique to the Ga tribe. It has been experienced and tested by millions upon millions of our ancestors across a multitude of cultures throughout history. As such, the theory and practice of mindful drumming, a modern application of this timeless wisdom, can be tested by your own direct experience, along with the ever-present possibility of inspiration from your own ancestral knowledge.

This is essential wisdom for today's world. The same universal principles which have been practiced by indigenous people over the millennia, and which I have learned from the ancestors, can be utilized by modern humans to inspire and invoke the unleashing of the human spirit. Those of us living in modern Western cultures can deepen our understanding of the processes of health and healing by embracing this natural path of wholeness and well-being.

Mindful Drumming

In the Introduction, I pointed out that *mindful drumming* is a very specific kind of drumming. I use the term *mindful drumming meditation* to distinguish between the powerful healing energy of repetitive drumming practices used in ritual by indigenous peoples and the sometimes random or chaotic use of drumming in less mindful situations.

The term *mindful* is familiar to many Westerners who have

explored the Eastern discipline and practice of meditation, which has flowered in the West particularly during the second half of the twentieth century. To be mindful means to be paying attention, deeply, fully, and with total consciousness. The Eastern meditative traditions employ a variety of methodologies to facilitate mindful meditation, including chanting, repetition of a mantra (a special word or sacred phrase), prayer, and simply paying attention to the rise and fall of the breath. All of these forms of meditation, if practiced long enough, can lead to an altered state of consciousness, or a trancelike state.

However, the mind is capable of creating endless distractions, and it sometimes takes many years of practice before meditators are able to enter into the deeper states of consciousness available through meditation. My experience is that the sound and rhythm of the drum facilitate these deeper states of consciousness and provide a reliable path into the meditative experience in a relatively short time frame.

With *mindful drumming meditation,* our focus is on the sound and rhythm created by the drum. This provides an effective means for unleashing the human spirit. Of course, this is not the only way to unleash the human spirit, and we will be exploring other methods in the course of this book, but I am presenting mindful drumming as the central focus because from my personal experience and from my observation of the many participants of my mindful drumming workshops, it provides an absolutely authentic and direct experience of universal truths.

In mindful drumming meditation, we start by playing a repetitive rhythm, eventually playing a series of diverse polyrhythms, thereby creating circular energy fields. The measurement between each rhythmic note must be equal in duration whatever polyrhythms are established, and I encourage you to repeat each rhythm for a minimum of three minutes before shifting to another.

Mindful drumming differs in some important ways from certain drumming circles which have become popular in some communities. From the start, the intention of mindful drumming is to create spiritual equilibrium, or inner peace and happiness. Therefore,

mindful drumming is best characterized as a form of meditation, not a form of "making music" or "jamming." As such, it is best for there to be no talking while drumming. Instead, everyone's intention is focused on *deep listening*. By this I mean paying attention with your heart and your whole being while drumming.

In mindful drumming meditations, one leader sets the rhythm, and simple rhythms are established and played for at least three minutes, then changed to create rhythmic circles of diverse polyrhythms. When we employ this technology of mindful drumming, either as individuals or as a community, a circular field of energy is generated. Ultimately, an altered state of consciousness is born. From this place, inner peace is established and restored. Mindful drumming meditation is fun and simple, and anyone can experience it.

The Many Benefits of Mindful Drumming

Mishe (Happiness)

One of the most important benefits of mindful drumming is *mishe,* my people's word for authentic happiness. According to the wisdom of the ancestors, happiness is bestowed upon us when we manifest here on planet Earth. By this I mean that each time a baby is born, s/he comes into being in a state of *mishe* in body, mind, and spirit. This state of happiness is inherent in the baby's very essence. It is always there, waiting within the child, available at any moment.

In contrast, in the United States and much of the Western world, happiness is viewed as something outside ourselves. In no less a source than the Declaration of Independence of the United States of America, the "pursuit of happiness" is extolled as an "inalienable right." But the idea that we must *pursue* happiness suggests that happiness exists *separately* from us, that it is something outside of our being which we must somehow chase down. When you consider that in one of the early drafts of the Declaration of Independence the phrase was "pursuit of property," which was then rewritten in the final draft as "pursuit of happiness," you can see that this idea of happiness existing somewhere outside ourselves is closely related to the basic premises of our capitalist economic system. Quite literally, we pursue "property," thinking having more things will bring us "happiness" as individuals.

Of course, in one sense, entering the marketplace does have something to do with happiness. For example, when we are feeling happy, we are often more susceptible to going shopping! I find that whenever I'm feeling fearful, my heart closes and reason tells me to stay home and keep my African eyes open and alert to trouble. I happened to be in Ghana, West Africa, visiting the land of my birth and shopping when I first heard about the terrorist attacks of September 11, 2001. This news shocked me deeply and paralyzed my ability to shop as I was engulfed with fear. Isn't it interesting that the president of the United States advised us after the attacks to get out and go shopping!

Well, it wasn't as easy as that, since our first task was to realign ourselves with spirit and experience our innate happiness. The way to get back to the state of *mishe* when we've slipped away from it, or even been torn away from it violently, is not through spending money; it's through engaging in spiritual practices such as mindful drumming that get us back in rhythm with our essential nature. No amount of money can restore and renew us and heal our wounding better than the application and practice of ritual through rhythm and sound.

The first objective of mindful drumming is joy and happiness. Anytime we play the drum, we are calling and inviting happiness. The most wonderful gift to wish for anyone is peace and love. In my Ga language, we say *"Hedzoleh aha bo!"* which means "Peace be with you!" Even if you didn't know the translation, these words could have a healing effect upon you. This beneficent wish is granted by spirit on a cellular level. So it is with mindful drumming.

I repeat: The deepest purpose of mindful drumming is to evoke *mishe*. We call upon the two forces in music, sound waves and rhythm—the goddess vibration and the god rhythm—to heal and uplift us. When these two are in harmony, we are able to remember who we really are, which is spirit. We are able to remember

that we are God. We are the Goddess. This remembering is made possible through mindful drumming.

Community Building

Another benefit of mindful drumming is that it helps us build community. Mindful drumming is a natural medium that inspires kinship and cooperation. It is so simple that you don't need special musical training to experience it. Anyone can participate. Mindful drumming can be done by one person, but it is ideally suited to be practiced by a community or group of people coming together to drum. In drumming together, drummers invoke *mishe ke sumo* (happiness and love), qualities we humans are made of but often seem to have forgotten.

In a group setting where people drum together, a reciprocal love affair develops that is quite contagious. People are inspired to share their *mishe* in a spirit of sisterhood and brotherhood. Once a true collective rhythm and sound is established, we are literally in rhythm and vibration with our neighbors. Violating this spirit of community by treating anyone unkindly becomes next to impossible.

Mindful Drumming as Meditation

As I indicated at the start of this chapter, mindful drumming is also a form of meditation, and it brings with it all of the benefits of meditation, including greater insight, deep relaxation, and improved health and well-being. Allow yourself to experience this in the following simple exercise.

PRACTICE TO UNLEASH THE HUMAN SPIRIT
EXPERIENCING DRUMMING AS MEDITATION

1. Once again, turn off your radio, TV, cell phone, beeper, and any other potential source of distraction. Get out your drum, or if you don't have a drum, imagine your thighs to be a drum, or perhaps use your kitchen table. Sit quietly in a comfortable position.

2. Bring your fingers close together the way swimmers do; your

fingertips should be touching, with your palms flat. Raise both of your hands approximately one foot above your drum, and slowly feel your hands falling on the drum. Play in time; this means that when your hands first land on the drum, you count one. Then, upon raising your hands, you count two, then three. Repeat this rhythm of one-two-three.

This rhythm is the beat of the German or Austrian waltz. It can be notated in the following way:

One – Two – Three / One – Two – Three / One – Two – Three
1 —— 2—— 3 — / 1—— 2 —— 3 — / 1—— 2——3——

3. Once you get into the groove, or the feel, of the rhythm, stop counting and experience the feeling. Let yourself go.

4. Play this rhythm for about three minutes, and then change the tempo (speed) from slow to medium. Now play and feel the rhythm for another three minutes.

5. As you drum, focus on any emotional challenges you may be facing at the moment. Allow yourself to sink into a deep state of meditation. Ask the rhythms and vibrations to assist you in reestablishing your inner peace.

Spirit, or *Mumoh,* and Invoking the Ancestors

Mindful drumming is also helpful in invoking the ancestral spirits, who can bring us guidance in many forms.

There are two instruments that are played by every culture that has ever existed. One, of course, is the drum. The other is the human voice. Both the drum and the human voice arise from *mumoh.* In the language of my people, the word *mumoh* means breath, and it also means spirit. Air is the medium common to both. Therefore, from the African indigenous point of view, sound, which emanates from air, is said to be spirit. *Mumoh* is known as God, or infinite spirit, and resides in the breath of the drum, characterized by its sounds and rhythms, which calls upon human beings to gravitate to

its energy field, and unleash their own *mumoh,* or spirit. This spirit is everywhere and in everything, and it can be invoked at any time.

Because spirit, or *mumoh,* is in all of us, on a primordial level we are all connected. For example, you and I breathe the same air, and the air vibrates. This connects us, as we share together in the ongoing process of inhalation and exhalation. This extends beyond humans, as we breathe the same air that embraces trees, other plants, and all the many animals who walk or crawl upon the Earth. Remember that air is constantly being recycled from plant to animal (including humans) to plant. The air also connects us to the ancestral spirits, since our very own ancestors once breathed the same air we breathe today!

Collectively and individually, the depth of our spirit, or *mumoh,* is unleashed through the practice of mindful drumming. Mindful drumming operates on many levels. It aspires to awaken the depth of our being. It uses rhythm and vibration as nonverbal mediums, as a mystical means for invoking spirits from the spirit world and allowing us to connect our individual spirits to that of the community spirit and ultimately to the spirit of our ancestors. My people believe that our ancestors may be invisible, but they are always present. In Chapter Two, you will learn more about how the Ga people view the living ancestors.

In indigenous African culture, the one thing we crave above all else is *waku* (family). The path of mindful drumming provides an awesome way not just to have fun but also to call and invoke our ancestors and achieve a deeper sense of *waku.* For the Ga people, the idea of *waku* extends far beyond our immediate blood relatives; it includes not only the nuclear family and our extended family of grandparents and aunts and uncles but also anyone who is invited into the family fold. For example, if I invite a stranger home and introduce him or her to my family, that person is immediately adopted into the family fold. My people are willing to take any risk because they truly believe in universal brotherhood and sisterhood. Our family network also extends to include those who came before us—our ancestral lineage.

Health and Healing

The contemporary spiritual text *A Course in Miracles* (published by the Foundation for Inner Peace) states that health is inner peace; this truth is also reflected in the second principle of Dr. Gerald (Jerry) Jampolsky's twelve principles of attitudinal healing: "Health is inner peace, and healing is letting go of fear." Attitudinal healing is an alternative mental health program which offers a blend of spiritual and psychological principles that can change people's lives. My wife, Aeeshah, and I run the Attitudinal Healing Connection in West Oakland, California, which is based on these principles.

I was first drawn to the principles of attitudinal healing precisely because they mirror the profound wisdom and guidance my people receive from the ancestors and the village elders. In my Ga culture, *hedzoleh* is our word for peace and love, and the drum is the instrument that calls us to *hedzoleh* and to the state of *mishe,* or happiness. In its deepest sense, healing always refers to a restoration of these inner states of *hedzoleh* and *mishe.* The healing power of mindful drumming arises from its capacity to take us back into a state of consciousness wherein peace and happiness become our focus and our function. Indeed, peace and happiness and love *are* our essence, and mindful drumming allows us to remember this.

So what is healing? Healing in this context is realignment of the body, mind, and emotions in harmony with spirit. Our oneness with spirit is actualized when we enter the state of *mishe.* Based on indigenous understanding, emotional and psychological imbalance, as well as physical imbalance, can be moderated and cured with rhythm and sound waves. This is possible because our heart, from a biological standpoint, is a rhythmic pump that not only distributes blood but also distributes vibrations, including the vibrations from our drums.

My people believe that when we are faced with making a decision, it is ultimately our heart that must decide, not our mental faculties. From this viewpoint, reasoning or thinking alone can never result in wisdom. Yes, our mind continues to reason, but it is our heart that brings matters to resolution. When the heart arrives at a place of peace, that is conclusive. Such an outcome must by its very nature be in alignment with peace and love, because the heart's ultimate goal at all times is to bring us back into our natural state of *hedzoleh* and *mishe*. The heart is always operating out of the cosmic laws that govern the universe (remember that *uni* means one, and *verse* means song); therefore, our hearts are always singing one song. Inherent in every song is rhythm and vibration. No matter the angle from which we approach this fundamental truth, we are always taken back to the same source.

Individual Healing

How does mindful drumming facilitate healing? Consider that when our hearts are full of sorrow, sharing this with another person who is empathetic helps bring us back into balance. For example, if I told a friend that my father had died recently and I was feeling sad, that friend would naturally sympathize with my sorrow and share my grief. That sharing would constitute a place of healing for both of us. So it is with mindful drumming. Whether we are sad or angry or fearful, when we allow ourselves to feel the steady rhythm of the drumbeat, we begin to come back into rhythm. This is the place of healing. Mindful drumming allows our hearts to enter into this state of unity and healing together.

Whenever we are out of rhythm from a peaceful and happy state, we are in jeopardy and susceptible to illness, either physical or psychological. As the late Babatunde Olatunji, an eminent Nigerian composer and drummer, points out: "Rhythm is the soul of life because the whole universe revolves around rhythm, and when we get out of rhythm, that's when we get into trouble."

Once you understand the principles and dynamics of mindful drumming, you will see that it provides an ideal alternative path to preventative medicine. Study after study demonstrates that stress either causes major illnesses to develop, or makes existing illnesses worse. Mindful drumming keeps us from developing the stress that can lead to both physical and mental dis-ease. One of the many benefits of mindful drumming is that it brings us into a state of mental, physical, emotional, and spiritual equilibrium. This can help us heal as individuals.

Fear and the Aging Process

Aging is characterized by sagging and wrinkling according to Dr. Nicholas Perricone. Although exercise and a good nutrition play a major role in slowing down the aging process, stress caused by fear expedites aging to such a degree that it can kill you! As Dr. Matthew Fox puts it: "Fear is the door to the human heart through which evil spirits enter."

When we are afraid, our ears close, all communication stops, and we are less friendly. Conversely, when we are happy, our outlook on life in general is optimistic. Happiness is the ultimate stress-buster! Because happiness, or *mishe,* is one of the most significant benefits of mindful drumming, I have found that mindful drumming ameliorates stress and evokes the essence of youthfulness. I have known drummers in Africa who dramatically exemplify this claim. They remain vibrant and youthful and full of vigor well into their eighties and nineties.

By engaging in the rhythmic medicine of mindful drumming, we can actually slow down the aging process and even heal and ultimately regenerate damaged cells. This is another positive side effect of practicing mindful drumming meditation available to every individual.

Community Healing

As I hinted at earlier, mindful drumming also helps foster health on the community level. When our mind is at that place of peace and tranquility drumming brings us to, we expand our natural ability to create something meaningful and good. It is close to impossible to get into trouble by participating in something harmful to others, such as armed robbery. Imagine how different our inner cities would be if mindful drumming were practiced in our communities on a regular basis! If we are consumed with peace and love and happiness, then peace and love and happiness are what we are driven to manifest in the world. In Chapter Six we will explore how the community spirit evoked by mindful drumming can play an important role in community healing.

Intimacy, Sensousness, and Sound

The sound of drumming in a community setting affects our senses strongly and ultimately ignites intimacy among participating drummers. The senses become open portals through the twin attributes of rhythms and vibration (sound). When the portals of the senses are open, we establish the tenets of kinship.

The vibration of the air involved in drumming expresses itself as a sensuousness that serves as a gateway to our sharing our vital life force. This is similar to what happens during lovemaking, when two people give each other the permission to be intimate. As my people say, lovers "feel no evil and smell no evil" when they are intimate with one another. So it is in a circle of mindful drummers; no evil can enter, and everyone is safe to experience the intimacy and sensuousness of rhythm and sound.

One participant in a mindful drumming circle put it this way, "I cannot remember ever feeling such unconditional love and heart sharing from so many people. I now feel hopeful for our future—for all of us, for our world. I feel stronger, clearer, and more positive. I feel more certain of my purpose." This state of love and friendship happens because of the exchange of rhythm and sound waves among the drummers.

Through Western Eyes: Words from Dr. Dennis Hill

As a medical doctor with a holistic bent who has spent much of my adult life exploring the mystery of how people find healing, I have been struck by the many positive gifts I have received from my experience in mindful drumming sessions. These include:

Empowerment: I felt stronger about myself as an individual because I was a participant in the joint venture of creating the drum music. I had never before thought of myself as a musician, so this was truly an empowering experience!

Cultivating deep listening: In order to participate with others in creating the rhythm, I had to listen carefully. I was forced to pay attention to what the others were doing, and to stop and restart if necessary, so that I was in rhythm with the group.

Tapping the higher power within: This is an entirely subjective experience, but there is no question that in the peak moments of the experience, I had the feeling that I was my best self, and connected in some significant way to everyone and everything around me.

Community building: Drumming together with others created a strong communal experience in me, and, on an even deeper level, evoked a remembrance of an ancient way of life. At times I could almost see us sitting around a fire in a primeval forest, drumming into the primordial night.

Inner peace: I was markedly more relaxed and calmer after the drumming sessions than before I went in. Time and the all-consuming rush of urban life had ceased to be such an all-important matter.

Deep happiness: I felt a definite sense of joy and accomplishment accompanying the experience of creating uplifting rhythmic music with other people.

Self-esteem: Although this is a difficult thing to describe, I felt as though my self-image was improved by the experience of the mindful drumming meditation because I was an integral part of a group effort which created happiness for myself and for the others in the circle.

Reflecting on these gifts of mindful drumming from the point of view of a physician, I am struck by how all of them are potentially healing and health-giving, whatever one's physical circumstances.

Accepting the Gifts of Mindful Drumming

Mindful drumming demands a deep sense of sincerity. We must truly become "as little children" to accept the amazing array of gifts it offers us.

Let me share a story with you that I find illustrates the difference between how children and adults deal with gifts in the American culture. Some time ago, I read an anthropologist's report stating that more unwrapped candy is picked up by waste management in New York City after Valentine's Day than after Halloween, even though probably more candy is distributed on Halloween than any other time! I suspect that this is true in other parts of the country as well.

I believe that the reason for this discrepancy is that Halloween, which retains some of its pagan roots, is more oriented toward children, and children sincerely and joyously accept the gifts of candy and enjoy them. Valentine's Day, in contrast, is more oriented towards adults, who accept their gifts to be polite but add to that a measure of guilt. The fact is that love and affection—the underlying motivation of the Valentine ritual—do not receive full expression in this culture, and many people participate out of a sense of obligation rather than joy. So when adults receive gifts of candy that they don't want and that they feel guilty about, in order not to cause any embarrassment, they accept the gifts but then think the right thing to do is to throw the candy where it belongs—in the trash bin.

Now, I'm not suggesting that you eat a lot of candy, especially if you're diabetic or overweight, but I do ask you to consider how to accept the sweetness of the gifts mindful drumming has to offer you.

Some time ago, I got to experience yet again one of the gifts that sound and rhythm offer. My wife, Aeeshah, and I went to a performance one evening over at the University of California at Berkeley. The late Fela Kuti, the renowned Nigerian bandleader, vocalist, saxophone player, and composer/arranger who has introduced a new form of music called Afro-Beat, was performing. On this occasion, Fela Kuti had three backup singers who were moving in what I would describe as a body prayer to the beat of the music. Their dance and the music transported me into trance. By the time the concert was over, my whole being was vibrating in response to the rhythm. As I returned home, I reflected that when any three or more people come together to engage in a similar rhythm in unison, they evoke a hypnotic state that can bring us *mishe,* or happiness.

Mindful drumming, along with the gift of happiness, offers us the gift of inspiration. *Inspiration* is a truly sacred word; the *Oxford Dictionary* defines as "a drawing in of breath; the act of inhalation." It is important to note that the Latin word *inspere* means "to inhale."

Here again, we are reminded that breath is life, and breath is spirit. This is like a circle: We are made of breath and rhythm and spirit.

So inhale deeply. Breathe in the gifts of your drum. Feel its rhythm, and hear its sounds. Take them in. Soon you will discover that mindful drumming offers far more than an idle pastime. It offers a path back home to yourself. It offers one of the most powerful ways to unleash your human spirit. It offers profound peace and a whole new way of life.

Take the next couple of pages to write notes of your experience or draw pictures.

NOTES

Chapter Two

The Timeless Wisdom of the Ga People

Nuu ko yeh
Nyokyele mli!
Nyokyele mli!
Nyokyele mli!

Nuu ko yeh
Nyokyele mli!
Ni atsor leh
Ataa Odono!

Ni etso orr odono!
Ni etso orr odono!
Ni etso orr odono!
Ni etso orr odono!

Ni atsor leh
Ataa Odono!

*

There is a man
In the moon!
In the moon!
In the moon!

There is a man
In the moon!
And he is called
Mister Odono!

And he plays his drum!
And he plays his drum!
And he plays his drum!
And he plays his drum!

And he is called
Mister Odono!

~ Traditional Ga lullaby

This children's lullaby speaks eloquently to who the Ga people are in relationship to the cosmos, the ancestors, and their community. It is the story of a loving and compassionate man, three feet tall. He is a spirit called Ataa Odono, or Mister Talking Drum, and he lives in the moon. His gift is to play the drum for little children at the full moon. The sound that comes out of his drum is said to take all worries from children's hearts and minds. This is why Ga children are always happy at the full moon.

When Ga children hear the song of Mister Odono, they sleep peacefully. I share this story to demonstrate how innate rhythm and sound are to the overall fabric of life among the Ga people.

Language, song, and dance play a huge role in the rituals of my people, the Ga-Adagbe tribe of Ghana, West Africa. In this chapter, I will describe some of the basic principles of daily life among the Ga people and Dr. Den Hill will share some of his experiences, all of which I hope will provide the background so you may more fully appreciate the roots of mindful drumming in my indigenous culture.

Through Western Eyes: Words from Dr. Dennis Hill

After our long flight to Ghana finally landed in the capital city of Accra, we arrived at an airport that could have been an airport anywhere; the halls, the rows of seats, and the people in uniform all looked familiar. But once we checked through customs and immigration, and got our bags, and walked outside the building, it was as if we had gone through a gateway to an entirely different world. Although it was late at night, what seemed to be a sea of people was undulating beyond the outdoor railing. The air was warm, and there was an earthy aroma in the air.

Then, in the midst of the crowd behind the railing, we saw a small woman waving warmly at us. It was Kokomon's eighty-five-year-old mother, who everyone calls Mother Lydia. Although Mother Lydia is a small person, she has a big smile and a large presence. We piled into the waiting van the family had arranged for us, and drove on our way out of the city. Near the airport, the buildings and houses looked pretty much like those you'd see in any big city. But as we drove further out, the buildings became smaller and smaller, and we saw more and more people, either walking, sitting, or gathered in some way along the roadway or outside their houses. It was late at night on a weeknight, but it seemed as though everyone in town was outside!

Eventually we settled into our accommodations in Kokrobite, a small village on the coast about forty-five minutes from Accra, at a resort called the African Academy of Music and Art.

On the weekends, the resort put on a variety of shows open to the public. There was a very entertaining mix of traditional and performance music and dance. What struck me most was that each member of the cast was not only a drummer, a dancer, or a singer, but everyone played all of these roles. Everyone was capable of singing, dancing, or playing the drum. I realized that each of these young adults had heard music all of their lives, from the time they were strapped to their mothers' backs, and even while they were in their mothers' wombs. Rhythm and sound were part of their very being.

The Ga People

Oral tradition claims that the Ga people are descendants of one of the lost tribes of Israel, or perhaps descendants of the Ebo tribe of Nigeria. Some of their ancient spiritual codes and conduct can

be traced to ancient Egypt. The belief in ancestral worship dates back at least as far as 5000 BCE, and many of the Ga rituals and festivals have parallels in these other cultures.

Ga Traditional Land

To the Ga people, the ownership of land is a foreign idea. The people belong to the land rather than vice versa. The Ga red-land is particularly flat and stretches along the Atlantic coast of Ghana, extending from Langma Hill to Tema, the Harbour Township in the East-land. The traditional Ga territory is bounded in the north by the Akuapem Mountains and in the south by the rocky Gulf of Guinea. The Ga people share boundaries with the Dangmes in the east and the Awutus in the west. At present, most of the Ga people live in Accra, the capital city of Ghana. On a clear day, there is a spectacular view from the Akaupem Mountains looking toward the capital city of Accra. During the rainy season, tropical thunderstorms shake and rumble the flat red earth, bringing messages of hope and renewal to the people.

Livelihood

The Ga people mostly derive their livelihood from fishing and farming. All work is communal. At an early age, boys works as apprentices under the tutelage of the village men to engage in farming or fishing. Before sunrise, the men and boys gather a net along with some fresh water and food into their canoe and set out into the warm Atlantic Ocean and cast their net. As the sun rises, they paddle back to shore and call upon more support to drag their net to shore. The boys and fishermen sing as they pull their net from the ocean with their catch of the day.

Their songs are more like chants and share the characteristics of mindful drumming practices. By this I mean that the songs have simple melodies and the lyrics are composed of short phrases that convey messages of trust, courage, and community. Sometimes they engage in a simple call-and-response format where one person sings a single melodic line and the rest of the fishermen answer with such vigor in body and spirit that it creates a loud sound and a great deal of excitement.

All of the fishing is done by the men, and then the women sell the fish on the beach and sometimes take the remainder of their catch to market. The women smoke the unsold fish in red mud ovens to preserve them and keep them from spoiling, and the smaller fish are dried in the scorching sun.

Farming is a family undertaking. The girls and women tend to the seedlings and the nurturing of the crops. Especially during school vacations, children go to the farms to learn from the elders the value of the land and how to work as a team. Children learn at a young age the value of community and the power of the group, including the adage that "many hands make light work." When the entire community works together for the good of the whole, no one is hungry, and no one is homeless, and everyone has family and a sense of kinship.

The Oral Tradition

The Ga people speak a language called Ga. This language is tonal in character, meaning a change in tone may result in a change in the meaning of a word, or a change in its part of speech or its tense. The people use a spoken word to describe different things by changing the tone of the word.

Inherent in the language of the Ga people are the basic spiritual codes of the people. The language tells the story of the people. For example, there is no word in the Ga language for *bastard*, because there is no child who is considered to be "illegitimate" or without a mother or father. Another example of how the language expresses the culture, which I have already shared in Chapter One, is the way the word *mumoh* means both breath and spirit.

The British reduced the Ga language to the written word as far back as the 1700s, but the written form does not capture the tonal variations that affect meaning. Since the Ga people are known for their capacity to love everyone and accept everyone, in that light they demonstrated their acceptance of the Europeans by embracing the written word.

The medicine men, however, knew that the Ga language could

never be accurately captured with the written word. Therefore, they continued to teach the children their ancient wisdom through storytelling, singing, and drumming. For the Ga people, the oral tradition remains paramount, and the ancestors know that a story is a messenger that will carry messages to the children of future generations. It is a spiritual practice and obligation of the elders to educate the children in this medium. The following poem by the mystic Sufi poet Rumi speaks to this wisdom:

> *A story is like water*
> *That you heat for your bath.*
> *It takes messages between the fire and your skin.*
> *It lets them meet, and it cleans you!*
> *A feeling of fullness comes,*
> *but sometimes it takes some bread to bring.*
> *Beauty surrounds us,*
> *but usually we need to be*
> *walking in the garden to know it.*
> *The body itself is a screen*
> *to shield and partially reveal the light*
> *that is blazing in your presence.*

> ~ Rumi

The Ga language is very melodic. Visitors who don't speak the language but who listen to a group of Ga people speaking often say that it sounds as if the group is singing the words instead of speaking.

My people give an even greater importance to actual singing. They say that songs convey messages to the spirit world more quickly and more powerfully than the spoken word. This assertion is true in part because of the marriage of words and sound inherent in singing. The Ga people sing for personal pleasure and also for purposes of divination or ritual. As I have observed in other indigenous cultures, the use of song in rituals is profound and infectious, and people always fall into a trancelike state, or an altered state of consciousness. For the Ga people, such singing is almost always accompanied by drumming.

The Living Ancestors

The Ga people show a profound reverence and respect for their departed ancestors. These ancestors have a real and present existence for the Ga people. According to this tradition, when people die—or "go home," as my people sometimes say—they do not lose membership in the tribe. According to African indigenous wisdom, the body may die, but the spirit doesn't actually die. Therefore, my people believe that membership in the tribe is eternal, and our ancestors are still considered to be part of the tribal community. They are a present and an accessible source of community wisdom. Anthropologists call this belief system *ancestral worship.*

Another way to understand the idea of the living ancestors is to think of your parents. In my culture, we believe that our fathers and mothers, whether they are alive or dead, have always loved us and will always love us and wish us well. Their love is always present and alive to us. Isn't that wonderful—knowing that no matter what we do or don't do, we are always loved? The chain goes further back. Our grandmothers and grandfathers also love us, whether they are alive or dead. We can invoke these ancestors any time we choose through experiencing rhythm and vibration when we drum.

In my culture, when people go to court, they are given two choices. They can choose to swear by the Holy Bible, or they can choose to swear by their ancestral spirits. Almost invariably, I have been told by Nana Oduru Namapau, the president of the house of chiefs for the Ashanti tribe, they choose to swear on the Bible, because everyone knows that when they choose the Bible, judgment is delayed, but if they choose the way of the ancestral spirits, justice is immediate! The belief in the ancestors is so strong that no one dares to defy an oath or contract they have made that was witnessed by the ancestors.

Rituals for Connecting with the Spirit World

The Ga language and the power of *mumoh,* or breath, act as ferries or horses that transport my people and connect them to the spirit world. A specific ritual for this is pouring libation and calling on the ancestors with an accompanying invocation.

In such a ritual, an elder will pour *akpeteshie* (a local liquid concoction made from sugarcane or palm wine) into a *kputua* (a cup made out of a dry coconut shell), and then speak to the ancestral spirits as the *akpeteshie* is poured onto the red earth. Typically, only part of the liquid is poured from the cup onto the earth, and the rest is shared among those present at the ritual. Sometimes water is used in libation pouring instead of *akpeteshie*. The ritual of pouring libation is administered at all ceremonies to invoke the ancestors. The intention of the ritual is to inculcate the minds and hearts of the people to remember their ancestors both in difficult times and on happy occasions.

You, too, can learn to call upon the ancestors. Pouring libation is a form of invocation, and you may voice whatever prayer or spoken wish you like as the liquid is poured. Just be sure to acknowledge your ancestors as part of the process. Let yourself get a taste of this experience through the following exercise.

PRACTICE TO UNLEASH THE HUMAN SPIRIT
POURING LIBATION

1. In a state of mindful attention, fill a glass with water.

2. Go into a garden, a park, or your backyard, and pour the water on Mother Earth. As you pour the water, call on your deceased grandparents or great grandparents (even if you never knew them), and make a wish. State your heart's deepest longing as a clear intention. Call on your ancestors with the understanding that the plants and the trees and the sky are your witnesses. Save a little of the water back to sip yourself as you complete the ritual.

3. Remember to ask for a peaceful and loving life, for if peace

and love are bestowed upon you, everything else will be possible.

Rites of Passage

Among my people, rites of passage are very important and are performed at every major transition point in life, starting from birth. I'll give you a couple of examples of such rituals. Rites of passage for boys begin seven days after birth, starting with circumcision and followed by a naming ritual. Let me tell you how it was in my case.

A Naming Ritual

In the Hammattan season of 1949, a little boy was born to Nii Korley and Ayorkor of the Ga tribe in a fishing village called Gamashie in Ghana, West Africa. It was in the month of December, when the hot dry air blows across the Sahara Desert toward the Atlantic Ocean. It was a Saturday morning, and the mood in this African fishing village was festive, for this was the last day of the old year and coming of the new year.

By oldest tradition, seven days from the day one is born, and following circumcision, the outdooring-naming ritual takes place. At dawn, after the crowing of the roosters, my parents, Nii Korley and Ayorkor, took me out into the family compound under the African stars and the moon, and gathered with all my extended family, including the entire village, to complete the naming ritual.

A medicine man named Atta Ajabah held me up and pointed me to the African sky and prayed. He then placed me on the red earth and prayed. I was made to taste first water, then *akpeteshie,* a liquid beverage of aged sugarcane. Finally, the medicine man poured libation to invoke the spirit of all of my ancestors. Then he said, "Eyes but no eyes, ears but no ears, may this child respect and honor our ancestors and all beings, and may the village people bless this child with these gifts: love and attention, trust, compassion, and kinship. This child came to this earth with black chunky hair, and when the African sun turns purple on his last days, may he leave from this earth with white chunky hair."

At the end of this prayer, the entire extended family responded, "Hiao" (pronounced *he-ah-oh*), which means "Let it be so." Three

words were whispered in my ears: "Korkwei," because I was third born by ranking order; "Kwame," because I was born on a Saturday; and lastly "Blonya," because I was born on New Year's Eve. One by one, the family members gave the medicine man money with a message for Korkwei, which symbolized their commitment to the well-being of the newborn baby in their community.

My full legal name then was Halifax Korkwei Clottey, and I was known by the nicknames from my naming ceremony, Kwame and Blonya. Years later, I became known by my musical stage name, Kokomon — meaning ancient one.

Rites of Passage for Girls

The primary rite of passage for girls among the Ga people takes place at puberty. The young initiates are confined to a room for seven days and nights, where they are attended by mature women who serve as mentors in preparing the girls to enter womanhood and assume the full and awesome powers of the feminine principle.

Upon graduation, these young women are dressed like goddesses. They wear headgear decorated with gold ornaments, and their earrings, necklaces, and anklets are made of imported beads and the finest gold. Their faces are covered with a strong foundation makeup augmented with face paints. They wear a two-piece *kente* cloth, which is a multicolored fabric woven in Ghana. One piece is used as a skirt, and the other is wrapped below their chest, thus exposing their painted breasts. They walk through the community, singing and doing a dance called *Otofo*, which includes vigorous movements of their limbs and pelvic region. The village celebrates their entrance into womanhood with great festivities.

Through these rites, adulthood is acknowledged, and the young women are ready to enter into the full responsibilities of womanhood.

A Multitude of Ceremonies

There are so many ceremonies in my culture, and in this book I can take the space to share only a few, but I hope they will give you a sense of how my people use ceremony and ritual, always accompanied by drumming, to mark the changing seasons and to give meaning and shape to our lives.

Humowoh Festival

From ancient times, our ancestors have performed a ceremonial festival called *Humowoh*, which means "Hunger tomorrow," or "Hooting at hunger." In many ways, *Humowoh* resembles the Passover ritual of the Jewish people. For example, during the festival, unleavened bread is served, the color red is marked on doors or gates (remember the mark that the Jewish people put on their doors so that they would be "passed over" by the misfortunes that God was wreaking upon the Pharaoh's people?), and a story of remembrance is told at a communal feast.

Oral tradition has it that a very long time ago, famine broke out among the Ga people. As a result of performing their awesome rituals and following the spiritual codes of conduct, in a later season the people had an abundant harvest. The people were so jubilant to have food after being hungry so long that they made a joyous noise and literally hooted at the hunger that had plagued them.

I remember that when I was a child, my favorite part of *Humowoh* was going to the cemetery where my grandfather was buried to feast with the ancestors. On the way to the cemetery, the beating of drums cleared the path and announced to the ancestors that we were coming. The drummers were drumming to call upon the whole village to walk to the cemetery for the ceremony. I remember that the style of the drumming for the *Humowoh* festival was similar to the mindful drumming practice I now teach others; that is, each drummer played a specific rhythmic pattern, and by repeating the rhythm, a circle of sound and rhythm was created. As we approached the cemetery, the village chief, Nii Ofankor, was walking at the head of the procession, and the drums called out, "*Agoo, agoo, agoo,*" which means, "Knock, knock, knock" and which suggests, "Whoever or whatever is on the path, clear the way as we journey to unite with our ancestors."

As a child, I particularly cherished breaking the unleavened bread at the cemetery with those who had gone before us. I remember

the chief of the village, Nii Ofankor, calling on the ancestors as he poured libation. As is often the case in Western legal tradition, he always made mention of the day of the week, which was Saturday, and he emphasized again and again :"Today is Saturday, Grandmother/Grandfather Spirit. Saturday, ancestors. Saturday, and everyone is here to witness this day."

As if we were fulfilling a legal contract, the chief used language stating that the people of the village had made an agreement the previous year that they would be back to break bread with the ancestors, and now they had indeed honored their word and come back. In honoring this contract, the villagers in turn asked the ancestors to do their part in providing blessings for the growing of crops, for safety in the community, for well-being of the children, and for abundance. And the chief reached the conclusion of the ceremony by saying, *"Tswa, tswa, omanye aba!"* This saying is used at the end of many ceremonies, and means "May prosperity be bestowed upon us!" or "May all our wishes be honored and brought to fruition!"

The village people responded with a resounding cry of *"Hiao!"* or "Let it be so!" Then the chief poured *akpeteshie* into a coconut cup, and everyone sipped from it. For this part of the ritual, everyone sat in a circle, and the cup was passed from one person to the next. Even if you chose not to drink the *akpeteshie,* by tradition you were supposed to hold the cup up to your lips, so that even those who did not wish to drink alcohol were surrendering to the call and becoming witnesses to, and participants in, the ritual.

Through Western Eyes: Words from Dr. Dennis Hill
Lunch with the Ancestors in Ofankor

During my stay in Ghana with Kokomon, we attended the annual *Humowoh* festival in Mother Lydia's village of Ofankor. Although the ceremony is not generally open to the public, we were allowed to attend as guests of Mother Lydia and the rest of Kokomon's family. As Kokomon's guests, we had been welcomed openheartedly into the family fold.

We assembled in the courtyard of the chief's compound and

exchanged formal greetings through the chief's linguist and our group spokesman. It is traditional to offer something to drink to any traveler, and the chief offered us soda and beer. Then he and his contingent excused themselves to prepare and dress for the formal ceremony. We relaxed in the chief's courtyard. Across the way, we observed a young man with a large pole as long as he was tall, rhythmically pounding dough in a stone bowl. Sitting nearby, a woman would reach into the bowl on each upstroke to fold and wet the dough. At first it looked dangerous for the woman to have her hand in the way of the pole like this, but it soon became clear that the man with the pole and the woman working the dough were in complete harmony with each other, and you could almost dance to the rhythm they were making.

Eventually, everyone was ready for the ceremony. The chief and his entourage were dressed in traditional bright red attire. Two drummers sounded the call. The villagers began to assemble and to proceed down the path into the bush where the village cemetery is located. Along the way, a man with an ancient flint-lock rifle would fire occasionally into the air. This, along with the powerful drumming, was intended to let the ancestors know we were coming to visit them.

At last we reached the cemetery. The chief did an invocation, calling on the ancestors, and pouring libation on the ground as is traditional. Then he, along with the drummers and the entire contingent, went around to each and every grave and offered specially prepared food to each departed ancestor.

As I looked around, I was struck by the realization that every single person in the village was in this place, having a good time together, from the youngest to the oldest, including teenagers. This kind of gathering would be very unusual in the United States, except perhaps at a family barbecue. And here we were at a lunch with the departed ancestors, in a cemetery, and the entire village was involved. It was quite an experience. I was humbled by the generosity of the villagers in allowing us to witness this ancient and sacred ceremony.

Incidentally, after the ceremony, which took most of the day, we gave Mother Lydia a ride back to the city. Our van dropped her off,

and then she had another five miles to walk to get home, which she insisted upon doing. She attributes her good health to walking just about everywhere she has to go. A few days later, as our van was driving through Jamestown, some distance away, we again spotted Mother Lydia on foot, going about her day. She seemed to be everywhere!

Fantasy Caskets and the Burial Ceremony

Among my people, the belief in an afterlife has inspired the creation of fantasy caskets. These caskets honor the spirit of the person who has died. They are intricately crafted, and each casket is unique. The casket may be in the shape of a lion, a beer bottle, a fishing boat, a lobster, an airplane, or even a Mercedes automobile! The craftsmen who build these fabled caskets decorate them with something that in some fundamental way represents the deceased's hobby, occupation, or primary interest. You do not choose your coffin while you're alive, because my people feel that this may lead to death. Therefore, your loved ones choose a theme and call for the construction of your coffin immediately after you have died.

It takes about a week after a death for the coffin to be completed, and during this time, there is an almost continuous funeral ceremony replete with much drumming. The ceremony is finished with the actual burial. For these ceremonies, villagers dress in brightly colored traditional clothing. They are not glum at all, for they know the spirit is eternal and that the living presence of the deceased will still be with them as a guiding ancestor.

Through Western Eyes: Words from Dr. Dennis Hill
Magic in Oshie

At one point during our time in Ghana, our group was invited to attend an Abundance Ceremony in Oshie, a small fishing village not far from the resort where we were staying. Our group was received by the village priest in his compound, along with other members of his entourage. After some formalities, including the traditional invocation of the ancestors, pouring of libation, and passing the communal drinking cup, we assembled alongside the village square, which was just a large open dirt area in the center of the village. We sat in a semicircle on chairs facing the square. Fetish priests and priestesses buried uncooked eggs and yams in the ground. During the course of this ritual, the eggs and yams would be cooked without fire.

Three drummers were to our left. They were supported by two men clapping hands, and one man playing a bell. Six fetish priestesses sat further around the square, all playing sticks to the infectious rhythms put out by the drummers. As we watched the ceremonial burial of the eggs and yams, quite dramatically and in a very short period of time a crowd of villagers gathered around the periphery. I felt something behind me, and when I looked around, there was a wall of children pressing forward to see what was happening. It was another example of the power of the drum call.

At one point during the afternoon-long ceremony, an elderly village man called me into the circle to dance with him. I didn't know the protocol, but Kokomon nodded to go ahead, so I doffed my hat and shoes and joined the old man in the center of the circle. He stared at me as he was dancing, and all I could do was stare back and move to the rhythm. We danced progressively toward the buried eggs and yams, then turned back and headed for the drummers. When we got in front of the drummers, we were to stop dramatically and then return to our seats. On the way back, I looked into the eyes of the lead drummer, because I wanted to see the master at work, but I found that his eyes were looking right through me, fixed on something far in the distance. It was obvious he was in a very deep place.

I also noticed that the energy of the drumming and the rhythm section seemed to focus the attention of the entire village onto the buried eggs and yams. The atmosphere around the village square was quite intense.

At the end of the ceremony, the eggs and yams were dug up by the village priest, then offered to us. They were completely cooked, so hot and steamy we could barely hold each morsel! Each of us visitors had a bite of the ceremonially cooked food, much to the delight of the villagers surrounding us. Again I felt honored to have been allowed to share in this ancient and sacred ritual.

PRACTICE TO UNLEASH THE HUMAN SPIRIT
MORE DRUMMING

1. First, turn off your radio, TV, cell phone, beeper, and any other potential source of distraction. Get out your drum, or if you don't have a drum, imagine your thighs to be a drum, or perhaps use your kitchen table. Sit quietly in a comfortable position.

2. Now, sing or chant this phrase, allowing yourself to feel its rhythm deeply: "I am! I am! I am that I am! I am! I am! I am that I am!" Then allow yourself to start emulating this syllables on your drum. It will sound like this: Koutun, Koutun, Koutun Da Koutun. Continue this rhythm for at least three minutes.

What We Can Learn from the Ga People

Along with the healing powers of mindful drumming, which you are already starting to get a sense of, what can we learn from the Ga people that will serve us in the modern world?

The principle of expanding our sense of family to embrace a larger circle is one answer. Another is that we can begin to act *as if* the intentions and commitments we set for ourselves are solemn oaths performed in the presence of the ancestors. Even if we do not believe in the idea of going to a cemetery and taking part in a ritual we may initially think of as ridiculous hocus-pocus, consider what we might gain if we truly honored our commitments and our intention to build an ideal community where everyone is honored and respected and takes the right action. Can you imagine how wonderful that could be?

That is why we so need the timeless wisdom of indigenous peoples. They teach us that the ancestors are always present. They witness *everything*. And they are constantly available to answer our deepest questions and longings.

Take the next couple of pages to write notes of your experience or draw pictures.

NOTES

 Mindful Drumming

NOTES

Chapter Three

The Role of Drums in Ritual

The gods themselves
will not enact ritual without us.
What actually makes ritual a requirement
is far beyond what the world,
as it is, can handle.
In the surface world,
our ability to make things happen
is very limited.

~ Malidoma Somé

Among my people, drums play a prominent role in all ritual and ceremony because the drum, on a primordial level, transmits messages from the people to their ancestors. The sound waves and rhythmic forms work as a vehicle to transport these messages through the drum. The Ga people view the drum as a sacred container, a vortex that holds all the wisdom of sound waves and rhythmic medicine, which we will be exploring more fully in Chapters Four and Five.

By their very nature, rituals and ceremonies require honesty, precision, and intimacy, and drums are ideally suited for facilitating these essential qualities in a simple and joyful way. In addition, authentic and powerful rituals require an atmosphere of safety and

confidentiality, which drumming provides. This is equally true whether we are in the setting of Ghana, West Africa, or of modern urban America. My wife, Aeeshah, and I have witnessed time and time again how drumming together creates just such a safe container in the circles we offer on racial healing, which we described earlier.

The African shaman and teacher Malidoma Somé, whose quotation opens this chapter, reminds us that "the gods themselves will not enact the ritual without us." We need a technology that possesses genuine spiritual powers of its own to facilitate the ritual process. This simple but potent technology is available to all cultures and embraces the basic characteristics of our humanity.

The basic characteristics I am talking about are our very own rhythmic pulse and our very own breath. The Ga elders teach that the drum possesses these same characteristics, through the power of sound waves (breath) and rhythm (pulse). As I have said earlier, the drum and our human voice are the two musical instruments that are prevalent in every single culture in the world, past and present. Drums, then, allow us to amplify the essence of our humanity, so that we may unleash our human spirit.

Ritual and Ceremony

Among the Ga people, all ritual is initiated through ceremony. There are two basic parts of any ritual: the visible part and the invisible part. There are three possible forms of ceremony: personal, family, and community.

For example, a personal ceremony might include you as an individual in the company of spirit and nature (trees, stone, river, and so forth). A family ceremony is performed within the boundaries of your close, intimate family. Among the Ga people, the rites of initiation overlap with family ceremony to become a communal experience. This is because the root of the community begins with the family. Community ceremony involves the whole village, along with nature and the ancestors.

The Making of the Drum

Remember, every culture in the world has some form of drum.

Thus, there are many, many different kinds of drums, made of a variety of kinds of materials and possessing different sounds and timbers. However, also remember that every single drum, whatever it is made of, contains the twin powers of sound (breath) and rhythm (pulse).

For the purposes of this book, I will be describing the drums from the culture of my people, which are made from wood, animal skin (usually the skin of a goat), and string. So that you can better understand the true power of the drum, and its essential role in ritual, I will share with you the birth of a drum from the view of the Ga people.

Selecting and Felling the Tree

First, in my culture, the selection of materials for a drum in itself deserves special attention. The *bosumfo* (healer) traditionally makes the choice in the species of wood for the carving of the drum. Only a few trees are considered, and it is important to note that the choice of the specific tree is a spiritual one. The tree is selected because it is believed to possess supernatural powers of its own. Indigenous Africans believe that all creatures are endowed with an immortal soul, including trees, plants, rivers, lakes, animals, and even the ocean. So the *bosumfo* tunes into the soul of the tree being considered for the making of a drum.

After the *bosumfo* has selected a particular tree ideally suited spiritually and physically to become a drum, before felling the tree the carver must appease the spirit of the tree. The ceremony to appease the spirit of the tree usually involves a sacrifice of eggs, fowl, or sheep. The first step is to ask the tree what is appropriate. The ritual sacrifice is performed under the tree. The animal being sacrificed is also asked to contribute to the ultimate healing work the drum will perform once it is complete. The blood of the sacrificial animal is used to consecrate the tree. Those performing this ritual do so with a deep sense of gratitude, which includes offering the pouring of libation to the animal spirit.

Once the tree is cut and the wood selected for the drum, the carver begins his work. Among the Ga people, drum making has

traditionally been restricted to men because of the enormous physical challenges involved. Drum making also demands exceptional skill, patience, understanding, and spiritual power. As I have described, the wood for the drum is selected for both spiritual and practical reasons.

Because the drum is a vortex and medium through which the voices of the ancestors are heard, the drum also serves as a canvas on which images of gods and goddesses, figures of chiefs and queen mothers, and sacred symbols of the cosmos are carved. The work of art created on the drum by the *bosumfo*, or healer, embodies both sacredness and beauty as the key to its invisible powers, which will unleash both the individual spirit as well as the community spirit.

Tools for Making the Drum

Only a few tools are used for making drums. The adze is an axelike tool that chips the raw pieces of wood and helps mold the wood into its intended design. The adze is also used to cut or split the wood. The drum maker also uses a flat piece of iron with a sharp edge similar to the blade of a carpenter's plane; a very sharp small knife; a species of spoke-shave (a blade set between two handles) for planing the wood; about four chisels; and an awl (a small pointed tool used for piercing holes), which is slightly bigger in diameter than the awl of a shoemaker.

The tools are stored in a special place free from the danger of desecration. The drum makers are extremely conscientious about their tools, being sure to avoid exposing anyone, especially any children, to any danger of being hurt by them.

Besides the ritual made to appease the spirit of the tree, drum makers also perform certain spiritual rites over the tools they will use in the carving of the drum. Before any carving begins, and sometimes when a job in process is not proceeding to the carver's satisfaction, the carver performs rites over the tools, which include the invocation and pouring of wine and the sprinkling of the blood of a fowl.

A Carver's Tale

This is a story told among my people. Long ago, there lived a man. Kofi Dua was his name. He was a wood carver and drum maker. The village people sometimes called him Nyame Dua, which means Tree God.

Just as it was in the time of his father and his grandfather before him, Kofi Dua made a traditional choice in the selection of the wood to be carved for each drum. He gave very careful consideration in finding a spiritually and physically strong tree, like the African lion. Kofi was not only pragmatic; he knew that the carving of each drum was a ritual in itself.

Each and every time Kofi went out into the jungle and selected a tree to be cut, standing under the tree he started his rites with this call:

> *Grandfather, grandmother spirit,*
> *here is a drink for you.*
> *Please receive this offering.*
> *Dear tree, I am going to fell you*
> *and make a drum out of you.*
> *Let no harm visit me now or afterward.*
> *Honor my highest intention*
> *for making this drum—*
> *and that is for this drum to be*
> *a healing instrument for*
> *many generations to come.*
> *Tswa, tswa, omanye aba!*
> *Hiao!*

With these sacred words, Kofi called upon the living ancestors, and by calling on the ancestors he enacted a ritual. Kofi knew that every drum carved demanded a special ceremony and a calling of the ancestors so that the drum would last a long time. He also knew he needed to design the drum to be light in weight so that people could carry it with ease. Kofi knew that the awesome spiritual power of each drum would enable his people to communicate with the

ancestors and be transported to the spirit world. Through the drum, the people would hear the voices of the ancestors. So making each drum was a spiritual act for Kofi.

Kofi earned the title *Okropong*, meaning Eagle, because Kofi had the power to transform himself and look through the eyes of an eagle to locate the trees that possessed supernatural powers and spirit. Kofi also transformed into an eagle because sometimes other spirits seek refuge in the tree, and it takes a carver with immense spiritual power and understanding to know the proper rites to perform in order to release a strange spirit from the tree. This is important and necessary, for if a drum is carved from a tree that is possessed with negative spiritual energy, it can evoke bad energy for the people. Kofi knew that there were only a very few trees that merited the honor and possessed the depth of supernatural power to become drums of healing.

The tree Nyamedua, whose name Kofi acquired when he became known as Nyame Dua (or Tree God), manifests great supernatural powers, and its wood is soft and white. This softness made it easier for Kofi to design and carve from it a beautiful drum. Kofi knew that trees best suited for making drums have the power to move themselves from one place to another. They can make themselves invisible to ordinary people if they sense that they are in any way in danger of being molested. The greatest caution must be exercised when dealing with such trees, and Kofi knew that making a drum from the wood of such trees was not a thing for amateurs. But Kofi was a master carver of great spiritual power, and he carved many powerful drums.

Connecting with the Power of Your Drum

As you can see, my people deeply honor all the steps that go into the making of a drum. Each step in its creation is accompanied by ritual and deep intention. Just imagine—the very drum you are touching also contains incredible spiritual powers. It contains the spirit and soul of the animal and tree that went into the making of it. It contains the energy, wisdom, and power of the drum maker. And it contains the supernatural powers of the ancestors and the spirit world to which it gives you access.

The next exercise gives you a chance to explore these dimensions of your drum with reverence and great conscious intent.

PRACTICE TO UNLEASH THE HUMAN SPIRIT
CONNECTING WITH YOUR DRUM

1. Once again, turn off your radio, TV, cell phone, beeper, and any other potential source of distraction. Get out your drum, and sit quietly in a comfortable position.

2. Hold your drum intimately, recognizing that the tree spirit and animal spirits are with you to assist you in creating a sacred space.

3. As you begin to play the drum, set your intention on Grandmother and Grandfather Spirit.

4. Gently spread both hands on the drum and begin rotating your hands in a semi-circular motion without leaving the surface of the drum. Feel the temperature and sensual texture of the animal skin. Listen to the gentle wind energy that forms as you navigate the surface of the drum with the palms of your hands.

5. Continue this semi-circular motion for three minutes, and then change it into a full circular motion for the next three minutes. Allow your heart to be open as you surrender to the wisdom of the spirits to release you from your fears. This way of playing the drum is effortless and fun. It evokes a high-level field of vibration, and provides an excellent vehicle for unleashing the individual and the community spirit. Have fun!

The Chief's Stool: The Power of the Drum in Ritual

Another tale my people tell concerns the incredible powers of manifestation unleashed through the conscious use of drumming in ritual. According to the story, the great master carver Okonfo Anokye possessed such awesome spiritual powers that he could become a hurricane and travel over seventy miles per hour, and the people and even great leaders turned to him for guidance and wisdom.

Oral tradition has it that there was once great turmoil among the Ashanti states. A meeting was called by Nana Osei Tutu, the great chief of Kumasi, to elect a paramount chief, or king, so that all the Ashanti states and chiefs could unite under him. This would mean that the elected chief's stool would be greater than all of the other stools, and that any chief enstooled by any of the states would have to swear an oath of allegiance to him. The challenge was: Who would be chosen?

At this juncture, Okonfo Anokye explained that the ancestors and the spirits would solve the problem. He would pray to the ancestors and the spirits, and at the end of the prayer, they would send a stool from the sky, and the chief on whose lap it landed would be selected the paramount chief. Okonfo Anokye asked everyone to fast and pour libation until the chosen day when the ancestral spirits would choose their king for them. Then they all dispersed to their various states. On the appointed day, which was Friday, the chiefs met, each waiting to become the paramount chief elect. Although the sun was scorching and hot, the atmosphere was calm.

Okonfo Anokye appeared amidst the drumming and the dancing of the ritual for invoking the ancestral spirits. After dancing a while, he began calling something from the sky as he looked upward. He continued his conjuring chants as the drumming increased. Then the sky became tense, and suddenly a stool studded with gold descended onto the lap of Nana Osei Tutu. As the chiefs had agreed, this meant that the ancestors had chosen Nana Osei Tutu as the unquestionable king of the Ashanti nation. Okonfo Anokye told the people that the stool contained the spirit of the Ashanti nation. And it was so.

Through Western Eyes: Words from Dr. Dennis Hill

The first time I saw authentic indigenous rituals was in Kokomon's homeland, but I had been introduced to the concept of indigenous ritual by Sobonfu and Malidoma Somé of the Dagara tribe from West Africa some years earlier in Oakland. I had learned that ritual is very important in village life, and that in Sobonfu Somé's village in Burkina Faso, nearly three-quarters of the time the villagers were either preparing for a ritual, performing a ritual, or talking about a recently completed ritual!

The elements of creating a ritual include community intention, the creation of sacred space by drumming, and an invocation to the deceased ancestors, creation of a shrine, and the active involvement of the entire community.

Even in our modern culture, I believe we can benefit greatly by participating in a ritual. We can create sacred space through our intention. In practical terms, we, the community gather together, then proclaim aloud that this space, or this circle, is sacred. Then that space or circle is "safe" for the community to conduct whatever ritual needs to be conducted.

The need may be the resolution of a conflict between two members of the community. Or perhaps the need is for a specific ritual or prayer for abundance, a memorial for the deceased, the celebration of a wedding, or any other community event.

It seems to me that in the West we have retained the vestigial form of some ceremonies but we have lost much of the magic of intentional ritual. In this, we have much to learn from indigenous peoples. In particular, I have come to appreciate the tremendous power of the drum in conducting a ritual. The drum calls the attention of the community members, drawing people together like a magnet. Once the people are together, they can get into rhythm with one another through more drumming, singing, or dancing.

A Modern Ritual

As I shared in the Preface, I first met Kokomon at the *Artship* dedication ceremony at Estuary Park in Oakland in 1999 where he and his wife Aeeshah did the opening drumming and invocation in a beautiful municipal park along the Oakland estuary a short distance from the famed Jack London Square. Several hundred people gathered for the event, and there were many booths providing food, art displays, and hands-on activities for the children. There were two performance stages for performing artists, including poets, drummers, and popular musicians.

But this ceremony didn't emerge out of nowhere. The preparation and planning process took several months, many committee meetings, and the involvement of dozens of people. The ritual intention was to rename the military ship *Golden Bear* the *Artship* and celebrate its new and peaceful community art purpose.

This is the way rituals are created. There is a specific intention declared, and then all the people involved work together toward that specific common goal. I will tell you a bit more about this special ceremony, as it provides a wonderful example of how we can incorporate some of the elements of indigenous cultures to create positive and meaningful ritual even in the most urban of Western settings, for Oakland is a city beset with all the problems that go along with large urban areas in the United States.

In this case, part of the process of creating the ritual was to build a shrine to the new purpose of the *Artship*. On the day of the event, the team I was part of built a framework using ordinary materials such as boxes and wood and covered it with bright traditional fabrics. Then a variety of objects, including handmade pieces of art and other personal items, were placed around and upon the shrine. At the top of this structure, we placed a scale model of the *Artship*. This shrine was placed about twenty yards in front of the main stage on the park grounds, with the estuary in the background. In creating this shrine, we took ordinary materials and placed them in such a way that they became special and extraordinary.

The shrine was the visual focal point of the ceremony. When the time came for the ceremony to begin, Kokomon, as I've described earlier, began playing his big traditional drum. The immense rhythmic sound caught everyone's attention and focused it in the direction of the main stage. This wasn't just a loud sound; it was a primordial rhythm pattern which touched something common in every person there, whether they recognized it or not.

Once the people were gathered and the rhythmic space was established, the drumming stopped, and Aeeshah stepped forward to do the opening invocation. She called on the ancestors and the spirits of the four directions to be present for this important event. Then the formal rededication ceremony begin.

The ritual portion of the ceremony involved fire. The idea was to use a torch, which represented the flame of the new and peaceful purpose of the former military ship. The ship was very dramatically towed into the estuary and held by tugboats behind the main stage, which was at the water's edge. This was an impressive sight, because the ship is an immense passenger liner. When the ship was in position, three drummers gave a signal, and a runner brought the Olympic-style hand-held torch which had been kept at the ready from the ship to the main stage and presented it to an elderly woman, who was there to represent the elders in the community. She, in turn, passed it on to a young person, representing the future. This young man then took it across the twenty-yard path to the *Artship* shrine and placed it in a receptacle there.

Around the shrine, young people representing all of Oakland's diverse neighborhoods were assembled. Each representative, ceremonially and in turn, stepped forward and lit a candle at the *Artship* shrine and then stepped back, symbolizing the sharing of the flame of community benefit from the *Artship* to be carried back to the various communities of Oakland. All the while, the drummers held the rhythmic space.

Along with poetry, there were also speeches by various dignitaries, including Oakland Mayor Jerry Brown and Nobel Prize winner Wole Soyinka from Nigeria. Before giving his prepared speech, Soyinka commented that the whole ritual reminded him of his own village in Africa. I took this as the highest of compliments. It seemed to validate the idea that, with proper intention and the power of drumming, even in a modern urban setting a timeless ceremony could be performed, drawing everyone in, and winning recognition from an African man as an authentic ritual.

Putting Ritual into Practice in the Modern World

You have now heard about some of the powerful rituals of the Ga people, and Dr. Den Hill has shared with you a description of a truthful and authentic modern ritual performed right here in the United States. Now I call upon you to begin to create and participate in your own rituals. The following two exercises can serve as starting points.

PRACTICE TO UNLEASH THE HUMAN SPIRIT
CREATING YOUR OWN BIRTHDAY RITUAL

1. Let us use a birthday ceremony as an example for creating your own ritual. Invite your friends and neighbors to join you for this special ceremony. The only tools you will need to perform this ritual are a drum and a glass of water. The glass of water will be used to pour libation, bringing an indigenous custom to your celebration. Ask one friend to serve as the drummer and another to pour libation; the person whose birthday is being celebrated is there only to receive energy from the group. You should not be the one to drum or pour libation!

2. Once your friends have arrived for the celebration, ask everyone to turn off all music, television, beepers, and cell phones. The person whose birthday it is should stand next to the drummer or the libation pourer. Ask everyone else to observe and participate by standing in a semi-circle.

Note: Keep this simple. Make sure no food is served until after the ritual is completed, and remind people not to talk during the ceremony, especially during the drumming.

3. Begin the ceremony by having the drummer play the drum slowly and steadily, in a style similar to the heartbeat (boom, boom, boom, boom). The drummer should listen for the sound to dissipate before playing the next beat. Have the drummer repeat this rhythm for approximately three minutes.

4. The person pouring libation will say the following phrase after s/he pours the glass of water onto the earth. "Today, [the day of the event], we have gathered here in the spirit of love, peace, and gratitude. To the spirits among us, to the spirits below us, to the spirits above us, and to all of our ancestors, please come and bless [name of person celebrating birthday] and [her/his] life and work. We ask for [her/his] happiness and honor in the community." Others can add more blessings for the person who is the recipient of this special occasion. When pouring the libation, only pour a small amount onto the earth or into an earthen cup, because the remaining water will be shared by all present to conclude the ritual. As the cup is passed from one guest to another, all hold in their minds the sacredness of everyone preset.

Reminder: Pouring the water in libation is a form of invocation; therefore, you may write your own prayer befitting the occasion.

5. End with the libation pourer stating: "*Tswa, tswa, omanye aba!*" (meaning "May we be blessed!" or "May all our wishes be granted and brought to fruition!"). Then the whole group will loudly proclaim, "*Hiao!*" (pronounced *he-ah-oh*), meaning "May it be so! Let it manifest!"

6. You may adapt this ritual for other celebratory occasions, such as honoring a couple who has gotten engaged or celebrating a new job or other accomplishment.

PRACTICE TO UNLEASH THE HUMAN SPIRIT
CREATING A RITUAL TO FRAME YOUR DAY

1. Transform your dresser into a sacred ritual altar. Get a small plant and a rock and place them in front of a mirror on your dresser. The plant and rock will serve as your witnesses.

2. In the morning, after taking your shower, go through your daily routine of dressing. Then, standing in front of the mirror on your dresser, say out loud, "In gratitude I stand here. Great Spirit,

bestow love and peace upon me this morning, and I, [state your name], promise to share these gifts with any being who crosses my path. *Hiao!* So be it!"

3. Repeat a similar ritual in the evening before bed, this time saying aloud, "In gratitude I stand here. Great Spirit, lift from me any challenges I have encountered during my working hours so that I may sleep in peace. *Hiao!*"

4. Use your imagination and creativity to adapt this ritual to suit your circumstances and inclinations. Be sure to include witnesses (which can be elements from the natural world, such as the rock and plant mentioned above). The possibilities are limitless!

Creating your own rituals both individually and communally is an empowering, life-affirming act which brings magic in its wake! Please consider making rituals an ongoing part of your life.

Take the next couple of pages to write notes of your experience or draw pictures.

NOTES

NOTES

Chapter Four

Sound and Vibration

Koryor,
Wind Spirit,
Invisible and mysterious.
Without you,
There would be no life.

Koryor,
Wind Spirit,
Flies without wings,
Moves without legs,
Inherent in
All things great and small.

Koryor,
Wind Spirit,
You are
Hurricane,
Tornado,
And thunderstorms.

~ Kokomon Clottey

Sound Waves and Vibration

Everything that exists vibrates. By *vibration,* I am referring to the creation of sound waves. Sound is produced by vibration. From the perspective of African shamanic tradition, sound, which is the subject of this chapter, is seen as possessing a female energy, complementing the male energy of rhythm, which we will be exploring in Chapter Five. Please note that vibration (sound) and rhythm are two sides of the same coin, two aspects of one whole. Nevertheless, to help you understand them more deeply, I will be focusing in this chapter on the feminine principle of vibration, and in the next chapter on the masculine principle of rhythm.

The elders teach that the female energy of sound (vibration) is infinite and all-embracing. It may manifest almost without our noticing, but it is always present and ultimately invincible. My people speak of sound in connection with wind. Wind may cause fires to burn out of control, or bring about the destruction associated with tornadoes or hurricanes. It can also manifest as the gentlest of breezes.

Human sound is created by air traveling through our vocal cords. Woodwind instrument produce sound when air is blown into them. My people believe that in the beginning *Mumoh,* or Spirit, created us in its own image. The primordial nature of Word/*Mumoh*/Spirit challenges us to examine the role sound plays in our lives. What does sound mean to us?

As the Christian Bible says, "In the beginning was the word [which can also be translated as breath or sound], and the word was God." The mythologist Joseph Campbell, who studied creation stories from cultures around the world, has written: "Creation in Hinduism depends on the five elements of ether, air, fire, water, earth. The first is ether, and ether is sound—the original sound, the nada. Out of the vibrations of nada comes the universe. That's the beginning of the universe—it begins with sound, with vibrations."

As humans, we are all sound makers, and in this way we are all like gods and goddesses. We create sound as air is expressed through our vocal cords and we sing or speak. We create sound in the form of vibration with every step we take. And, in the context of mindful drumming, we create sound as our hands come into contact with and make an impact upon the animal hide on the surface of our drum. This impact generates movement of air, which travels through a chamber of hollow wood to push the air to vibrate, creating sound waves, from which the sound of the drum is born.

Creative Vibrations

Even modern science looks at the "energy" inherent in the creation process in terms of sound waves. According to the big bang theory, the universe is about 15 billion years old. What an astronomical figure! The contemporary physicist Gary Zukav has written of parallels between quantum physics and the sacred mystical traditions. He shows how vibration, or sound waves, acted on the primordial level as a catalyst to set in motion the beginning of creation. From the very beginning, sound waves brought everything that is into existence and bestowed upon us the underpinning for our creativity as well as our survival.

Gary Zukav has also written about "emotional currents," using the metaphor to describe currents studied by science, such as electricity. I like the phrase *emotional currents* because it paints a picture that provides a way of looking at vibration. As I've said, everything vibrates, although it is also important to understand that things vibrate at different frequencies. For example, the Golden Gate Bridge in San Francisco vibrates all the time, even if we cannot see this vibration except when there's a very heavy wind. Trees and plants vibrate. Animals vibrate.

The modern science of sound therapy describes the process of *entrainment,* wherein the lower frequency sound can pull others toward its slower vibration and greater amplitude. Vibrations, in this way, spread from one source to another; in other words, they can entrain nearby vibrations, bringing about a shared state.

On the human level, we can appreciate the power of vibrational entrainment by considering the example of a woman meeting a man and falling in love. The palpitation of her heart and the feelings that emanate and flow from her heart make it so that she cannot deny the feeling of love. The sensation may be so powerful that it is almost painful. The sweet feeling of this state of being in love is infectious. At a wedding ceremony, for instance, the room may become so engulfed with the vibrations that those present find their hearts filled with love and their eyes brimming with tears.

This is the work of vibration (sound waves). Such an energy field is infectious. It spreads to others much the way the energy states of quantum mechanics are conveyed—instantaneously.

Good feelings are literally catching! When I am so happy that you detect real sincerity in my happiness and laughter, you will be inspired to laugh. What causes this inspiration is the transparent energy field that transmits emotional states as vibrations. Good vibrations, or "good vibes," create a very sensual and spiritual experience. If you meet someone, even a stranger, and feel the love, grace, and compassion that travels from that person's heart to your heart or from your heart to the person's heart, one of you may say, "I'm getting good vibes from you!"

When you resonate at the same frequency of vibration as someone else, an emotional current is born so that you come to a place of oneness, or shared rhythmic space. This is, quite simply, a heart connection. The very chemical balance in your bloodstream shifts, affecting your entire body, including your brain. This inspires your love consciousness, and all sorts of miracles start to happen. This kind of happiness takes place within an energy field, and the energy field in this case is the love vibration.

The Sacred Spoken Word

Spiritual traditions throughout history and across all cultures have honored the power of the spoken word. When I was a child in Africa, my elder brother Mohammed initiated me into Islam. I was taught not only to pray five times a day, but also to speak aloud to Allah in all my deliberations. This way of worship felt in harmony with the rituals of my people, such as the invocation of the ancestors while pouring libation. According to this perennial spiritual code of conduct, we speak out loud our highest intention of peace and love to our ancestors and to the earth community. This form of prayer performed in the context of ritual is immensely powerful.

The sound that comes out of our being when we open our mouth is sacred because it is made of sacred breath. Without this breath, we would cease to be alive. In our daily lives, both personal and professional, we need to speak in order to communicate our intentions and our thoughts to our loved ones and our business associates. Today's technology makes it possible for us to transmit the power of the sound that emanates from our sacred breath over vast distances via the telephone. And the mass media of radio and television even make it possible for the spoken word to be heard by billions of people all around the globe. But even with all the powers of technology, the beginning point is still sacred breath and the spoken word.

Communication

Throughout human history, words have allowed us to communicate with one another. And even before there were telephones, there was another means of communicating over distances: In ancient times, messages were sent from village to village by drum. By playing a drum with low resonance, the Ga people would send a message to let the people know a ceremony was about to take place. They still practice this form of communication by drum today, and always it seems that the children are the first to hear this message. They then become the human messengers and run to spread the word to everyone else.

Sound waves also provide the most expedient media for sending messages to and receiving messages from the ancestral spirits. As we play the drum, our message is sent to the living ancestors. Among the Ga people, the ancestors answer by possessing mediums, or channels, and this is how they make their voices heard.

There was a medicine man in my village who worked with *adopeh* (called leprechauns by the Irish) as messengers. He said that the *adopeh* were his friends, and aided him with understanding herbal medicine. When he was faced with a very serious problem, he would send his *adopeh* friends to fetch the medicine necessary for performing his rituals. At times, however, this medicine man would

travel directly like the wind to the ancestral spirit world to strengthen his powers.

Sound is used by such shamans as the gateway to the sacred portal of the ancestors. My people call the wind *Koryor* and view it as invincible and mysterious. Without *Koryor,* life as we know it would cease to be. *Koryor* is feminine and gentle, yet at times *Koryor* can create a tornado or hurricane. Let us remember that this energy can be accessed at any time to communicate our intentions to our ancestors and also to unleash the human spirit!

The Sacred Sound of Song

Vibration may take the form of speech, and, even more powerfully, it may take the form of song. The sounds that we create by singing sweet melodies or by playing wind instruments, pianos, guitars, or drums all, in the broadest sense, emanate from the very core of our being.

The Musical Scale

Vibration can be seen as an ocean with many rivers that lead into it. One such river is the musical scale. In Latin, the word *scala,* the root of our English word *scale*, means step. The musical scale is a series of steps made up of notes, each of which vibrates at a different rate. Scales provide the foundation for melodies and the harmonic structures for musical arrangements.

Songs can have a profound effect on our emotional state, and musical arrangements can be orchestrated intentionally to teleport us to the state of *mishe*, to facilitate us in experiencing happiness. Other arrangements might trigger sadness, anger, or bliss. If, like the Ga people, we consider vibration to be a goddess and rhythm to be a god, then the union of these divine beings can bring about the sacred birth of *mishe*. This is the medium by which mindful drumming operates.

As we drum and generate sound waves, the vibration is absorbed not only through our ears but through our entire body and our whole being. My people say: Listen with *all* your senses, with your full attention. This is *deep listening.* When you listen deeply when you are drumming, the process of renewal and rejoicing is palpable. This experience is particularly potent when you are drumming with other people.

Through Western Eyes: Words from Dr. Dennis Hill
Sound and Vibration

Before I encountered African drumming, my firsthand experience with the power of sound and vibration came from Buddhist chanting. I have been practicing Buddhism in the Soka Gakkai tradition since 1988, sharing in the gifts of this ancient tradition which have traveled from the Far East to the West. My practice includes mindful chanting of a sacred phrase twice daily, morning and evening, in front of a simple Buddhist altar. When I first started this practice, I mostly chanted by myself, and I received wonderful benefit from it.

I noticed, however, that when I chanted with other people the experience was even deeper and more rewarding. A powerful communal feeling was created as we repeated the sacred phrase over and over again. Each of us was doing the same chant, in harmony with one another, and sustaining the chant over time.

As I would later experience with mindful drumming, a bond would form out of the shared rhythm we created together. Even when chanting with strangers, I would notice that forming meaningful relationships was easier because of the community we'd experienced through sharing sound and rhythm. As a result, I sought out people to chant with. I credit this practice with helping me overcome my solitary nature and rejoin the world of people. This was ever so much easier than trying to "make conversation" with strangers at an ordinary social gathering.

As Kokomon has said, repeating a spoken phrase over and over, like repeating a rhythm on the drum over and over, creates a circle, a contained rhythmic space. This provides a direct path to spirit. Whether we are using a six-syllable Buddhist mantra or a drum, this circle creates a sacred space, a place where we can feel spirit, or what the Buddhists call our Buddha-nature within, and observe our ordinary state of mind from a compassionate distance.

In Kokomon's culture, I have come to understand, every person is considered to be a spirit in human form. This corresponds to the Buddhist teaching that each of us is a Buddha. The Buddhist scriptures teach that we are common mortals only because we are deluded concerning the fact of our Buddha-nature. People who have realized and appreciated that they are Buddhas tend to treat everyone else with the deepest respect and compassion, because that is the behavior of a Buddha. People who are treated with respect tend to respond with respect.

Another passage from Buddhist scripture states that if one bows to the Buddha in the other person, the Buddha will bow back, just as if it were an image in the mirror. When I traveled in Ghana, I experienced this essential truth in each personal interaction. I felt acknowledged as an individual spirit. The perennial wisdom flows through each of the world's great traditions, including the shamanic traditions of indigenous cultures.

Tapping into the Power of Breath (Spirit)

Sometimes children can be our greatest teachers. They pass the ancestral wisdom to us directly and without pretension. I can well remember a time a child I know showed a primordial understanding of the importance of breath. One cold October evening, as we sat down to our family meal, my wife, Aeeshah, asked our two-year-old granddaughter, Munirah, to pray before we ate. Munirah looked earnestly at those of us gathered, and then she blew a gentle cool air across the table. Her mother, whose name is Amana, and everyone else at the table thought that perhaps she was cooling her food, which was still quite hot, or that maybe she hadn't understood the request that she pray before dinner. So Amana repeated the request: "Munirah, please offer the prayer before we eat."

Munirah again blew a gentle cool air across the table, but this time she stretched out to reach as far as she could and repeated the process as she blew gentle air for each person at the table. Let it be known that Munirah already could speak very well for her age and never had any difficulty in communicating what she wanted! As such, we all finally understood her message of grace and prayer.

She demonstrated that we can hold an intention and not have to speak at all. We can just gently blow our prayer in the form of air. That is, in our communication with spirit or our ancestors, we can either speak or simply blow air as we hold our highest intention of peace and love.

Here is an ancient and innate wisdom that needs to be recognized. Munirah had performed a spiritual ritual that was nonverbal, deep, and profound. I was struck by her sharp perception and ability to invoke our mystical ancestral past. Young children often show this close connection to the spirit world, which we adults have largely forgotten.

Nadi shodhana (purification of the channels) is a simple exercise from the yogic tradition of *pranayama* (breath control; regulation or control of life force). It is intended to purify the *nadis* (channels) through which *prana* (life force), or breath, flows. It balances the flow of breath in the nostrils, and thereby the flow of energy through the body. It is an excellent exercise to practice anytime before you begin drumming because it puts you in touch with *mumoh,* the energy of spirit. Although this particular exercise doesn't come from the Ga tradition, it reflects the deep respect my people hold for the sacred power of breath. In my African homeland, people always breathe deeply as they drum or perform ritual. This exercise can help you do the same.

PRACTICE TO UNLEASH THE HUMAN SPIRIT
ACCESSING *MUMOH* THROUGH *NADI SHODHANA*

1. Turn off your radio, TV, cell phone, and beeper. Sit upright on a cushion or on a firm chair with your head, neck, and body in alignment.

2. Breathe in a relaxed fashion from your diaphragm for three complete breaths. Keep your inhalation and exhalation at an equal length, and allow your breath to be slow, controlled, and free of sounds and jerks.

3. After taking a deep breath, close your right nostril with the thumb of your right hand, and exhale completely through your left nostril. At the end of this exhalation, close your left nostril with your right index finger, and inhale through the right nostril.

4. Repeat this cycle of exhalation with the left nostril and inhalation with the right nostril two more times, always making sure to maintain an equal rate of inhalation and exhalation. At the end of the third inhalation with the right nostril, exhale completely through the same nostril while keeping the left nostril closed. At the end of the exhalation, close the right nostril and inhale through the left nostril two more times.

5. Now place your hands on your knees and exhale and inhale through both nostrils for three complete breaths. This completes one cycle of *nadi shodhana*. You may repeat this as many times as you like, either as a practice in and of itself or before you begin drumming or engage in any other meditative practice, such as chanting or simply observing the inhalation and exhalation of your breath.

Through Western Eyes: Words from Dr. Dennis Hill

There are many natural sounds and vibrations in the human body, and they are going all the time, twenty-four hours a day. Every human body is a rhythm-making, constantly vibrating entity. Some obvious rhythms are the heartbeat, the breathing rate, and the brain wave pattern. Some not-so-obvious rhythms are the contractions of the bowel, the bladder, and the other organs. The bottom line is that we all have an innate experience of rhythm. We don't have to learn it.

The challenge for people in our culture is to realize we already have this rhythmic foundation. It is part of our nature. For some reason, our modern world has made it less important to be in touch with this part of our being, but in the African villages I visited in Ghana, drumming, dancing, and singing are all part of everyday life—and each is a sacred expression of the spirit within.

Kokomon's mindful drumming meditation is a gift to us from

that culture, a reminder to modern people that there is an ancient way to get in touch with the primal, communal, rhythmic self, and to feel the joy of connection with other people in the community. I have had the great fortune to see and experience that a whole community can be transported together to that happy, mindful state that Kokomon's people call *mishe*.

Biofeedback

For just a moment, I would like to touch on the concept of biofeedback. This is an area of medical research where certain parameters such as the heart rate, blood pressure, skin resistance, or other indicators of stress and relaxation are measured electronically and displayed on an instrument, or audibly played back so that the patient can, over time and with practice, learn to change the readings to a more relaxed state by the mere act of observing the readings, or listening to the audio playback. The success of biofeedback in treating a large array of health problems shows that just by observing what is, there is a trend toward the more optimal relaxed state.

As a doctor, I've been fascinated to observe the way drums, or the voice in chanting, can be used as biofeedback devices. In fact, they are probably the very first biofeedback devices, since they have been around as long as humans have been around!

As we mindfully listen to the sound of our own drum or our own voice, we can, just by listening, gradually move to a more peaceful, yet focused state. In this state of heightened awareness, this "altered" or trancelike state, the mind is open and receptive. Unlike our ordinary state of mind, at least in Western societies, which is more oriented toward thinking, planning, controlling, and analyzing, this mindful, relaxed state can give us a rest and a welcome shift in perspective.

The Healing Power of Vibration

Dr. Den Hill has just pointed out some of the ways in which vibration and rhythm can heal us. Apart from the contemporary technology of biofeedback, vibration can share its healing powers

through the most basic of activities. Here, my editor and friend Nancy Carleton shares her experience:

The Healing Power of Vibration:
Words from Nancy Grimley Carleton

Not too long ago, I suffered a stress fracture at the base of the fifth metatarsal of my left foot. It was extremely painful, and after a humbling week on crutches, I went for an appointment with my orthopedist. I was surprised when he told me I could start putting weight on the foot that afternoon, since the current practice is to "get people back on their feet" as quickly as possible.

At first my foot hurt like bloody hell, and I hoped that the doctor really knew what he was recommending! But after only a few weeks, I found I could walk around my house and do quick errands fairly comfortably, if at a slower pace than usual. However, I was really missing my longer strolls, since ordinarily I walk around four or five miles a day.

When the third week passed, the orthopedist gave me permission to get back into the routine of my longer walks. The first time I walked a mile, I had an amazing experience. After ten minutes of walking, I became acutely aware of the vibrations traveling up my legs from the ground where my feet were hitting the pavement. A pleasant warm, tingling sensation accompanied this sense of vibration. By the time I completed my walk, I felt less pain than I had since the initial fracture, and I could feel my foot growing stronger with every step.

I had to recognize the wisdom of allowing these natural vibrations to help my bone in its healing process. Since then, I've remembered reading about how the vibration caused by walking, running, and other weight-bearing exercise is part of what builds bone in all of us; the vibration sends a signal that causes bone to form. It's just that most of the time, we aren't tuned in enough to experience the full sensation of the vibrations we create with each step we take.

The Power of Vibration

In the next chapter, I will be discussing the marriage between vibration and rhythm, which is truly remarkable. However, vibration alone, even without an intentional rhythm, can transport us to a place of sincere joy and happiness. Even if we are filled with grief and sadness—for instance, if there has been a death in the family and we are in a mournful and lugubrious state—vibration can carry us to a different place. By experiencing diverse sound waves we can be transported back to a state of *mishe,* or happiness. When the vibrations are strong enough, it is impossible not to succumb to their awesome force. It is in the very nature of our human spirit to resonate to sound.

Take the next couple of pages to write notes of your experience or draw pictures.

NOTES

Chapter Five

Rhythm

*Every footprint leaves
its mark
in the sands of life.
Step by step,
each one tells
a story.
Beat by beat,
echo
voices of the ancestors.*

~ Kokomon Clottey

The Energy of Rhythm

According to the wisdom of the Ga elders, rhythm is seen as possessing a male energy, complementing the female energy of sound, or vibration. Whereas the female energy of sound is infinite and all-embracing, the male energy of rhythm is precise, focused, and finite. When we are little children, we learn to walk, and our Ga elders teach us that we establish a unique and rhythmic step, and the number of our steps in this lifetime is finite.

Our individual rhythms also leave footprints in the sands of time. At Dinosaur Ridge in Colorado, the footsteps of dinosaurs who walked the earth 100 million years ago are preserved. The rhythm of their footsteps left an impression in the earth that has lasted all those millennia. Of course, sound always accompanies rhythm. Imagine the sound those gigantic dinosaurs must have made as they walked. But today we can only see and measure their footprints. Let us make no mistake that footprints are the descendants of rhythm!

Our Rhythmic Code

The Ga people believe that our individual rhythmic code can identify us from all others as precisely as a fingerprint. It can even be used to determine whether we have committed a crime. When we get into trouble, our rhythmic code changes. Many parents have experienced this. They leave their house to go out for the evening, and when they return they may sense if one of the children created a problem while they were out. If they can't get the children to tell them which one did it, there is a sure way to get at the truth. In the Ga culture, we would line the children up and ask that each child walk toward us. The guilty child's footsteps would be out of rhythm. By this I mean that his or her rhythmic code would have changed so drastically that it would be reflected in his or her spiritual, emotional, and physical fabric.

An experience I had as a child demonstrates this reality even more dramatically. When I was around ten years old, my mother took me to a village called Lakpleku. This village was known as a source of divination and the uncovering of mysteries, and often people went there to settle disputes or to hold trials to figure out who had committed a crime.

On this occasion, the scuttlebutt was that someone had committed a crime using paranormal powers which had resulted in the death of a child. The villagers of Lakpleku dealt with this by digging a hole in the ground about six feet long. It looked like a grave, and inside the hole was an opened padlock that was about six inches in diameter.

All those suspected of committing this horrible crime were

assembled on the south side of this very big hole. There were four men and two women. On the north side of the hole, there were six men with drums and a medicine man. The drums were enormous. The drummers began to play syncopated rhythms, and periodically they would stop, quite abruptly. As the intensity of the drumming increased, I noticed that the padlock was closing bit by bit.

Suddenly, I noticed that one of the men on the south side of the grave was beginning to tremble. It appeared as if he was being pulled by some unseen force. He struggled to be still, but it seemed as if he could not stop himself. The sun was burning hot, and the drumbeat intensified. The rhythms and sounds of the drums seemed to be having a hypnotic effect on the man, who was now trembling violently. The rest of the people who were on trial stood motionless and calm as the drums beat steadily and rhythmically.

I sat watching as the trembling man was pulled by this unseen force onto the red earth and was thrown into the hole. Just as he was going down into the hole, he screamed out his confession, but it was too late to save himself.

This may sound unbelievable, but as a child I saw it with my own eyes.

Through Western Eyes: Words from Dr. Dennis Hill
Rhythm Is Everywhere

Rhythm is in all things—quite literally in all things. From the subatomic level to the great cosmos itself, the common denominator of all things is rhythm. Electrons orbit nuclei, the planets revolve around the sun, the seasons of the year come and go, the heart beats, the lungs expand and contract, and all of this repeats over and over. This is rhythm. All of the universe is rhythm. All of life is rhythm. Once we realize this point, then we come to understand that the key to happiness, or *mishe* as Kokomon's people call it, is to be in rhythm with all life.

Over the ages, humans have developed specific methods for getting into rhythm with all life, which can be called spirit. Ancient cultures used singing, drumming, and dancing as a means to this end.

As I've shared, my own experience with mindful Buddhist chanting has helped me understand this principle. Through chanting and through drumming, I found I could get into a blissful state of mind. In that place, I could feel that I am indeed a vital part of all of life. I could begin to appreciate my own life from the deep perspective of the human spirit. This is a delightful place to be! To appreciate one's own life is the greatest pleasure. When we feel this way, we can appreciate others' lives as well. Indeed, we can truly appreciate all that life has to offer.

Children's Play

My experience in Kokomon's Africa spoke to this truth as well. The day after our arrival, Kokomon's Mother, Mother Lydia, came to visit us along with several other adult family members and friends, including about twenty-five children, ranging in age from about six or so on up to early teenagers. Mother Lydia brought traditional food, which we all shared together in a communal feast.

Following our feasting, we spent the afternoon together in a low-key way, with the adults sitting around talking or just relaxing while the children entertained themselves with their own games. I noticed that all of the children's games were based on rhythm. They happily engaged in call-and-response singing, body movement, and clapping as they stood in a circle. Each and every child participated, from the youngest to the oldest. There was no competition, and no winners or losers. Everyone was always included.

The children kept playing and entertaining themselves for hours while the adults watched from a distance. There was no crying, no incessant demands for something to do, no boredom, and the day passed in a leisurely and pleasant way. There was clearly a unity created by the rhythm-based games the children played.

Later, when the young adults at the resort did a performance for us that included drumming, singing, and dancing, I could see that the rhythm of the dance, combined with the rhythm of the drum and the rhythm of the voices, brought all the participants, including those of us in the audience, together into a unity, a oneness. The Buddhists call this sate of unity *itai doshin,* which means "many in body, one in mind." In this state, we transcend individual differences and attain true community. The Ga people experience this state on a daily basis.

Urban Reality

In contrast to that ancient way of being together, in our modern world we are generally separated from the rhythms of nature and the instinctive desire to sing, dance, drum, and express ourselves. Our fast-paced lives leave little time. Our freeways, large buildings, and concrete urban design tend to separate us from nature and from one another.

When we do get some free time, we tend to pay money to go see someone else sing or dance, or we sit at a sporting event or in front of the television set waiting to be entertained. We may move a little in our seats, but generally we are passively observing *someone else* performing. This is not a true rhythmic experience. To get the full benefit of rhythm, we have to do it ourselves. We need to get up on our own two feet and move! This process doesn't require us to be "good" at dancing; it doesn't require that we be "good" at singing or drumming—only that we be willing to get up and express ourselves!

Although we live in a fast-paced world of many distractions, we can still benefit from the ancient methods of getting in touch with spirit. We can set aside some time on a regular basis to do some mindful drumming. Again, mindful drumming doesn't require that we be "good" at drumming. It only requires that we be truly mindful, that is, that we listen deeply to the beat and allow ourselves to come into rhythm with the other drummers.

We can also do mindful drumming by ourselves at home and derive benefit from the experience. The preferable way, though, is to drum with other people; then we can come to a place where we are in touch with our own human spirit, and in touch with the human spirit of others. When we are in this place, we experience an indescribable joy. We are not alone; we are together as one in human spirit.

Gateway to the World of Spirit

Rhythm serves as a catalyst and as a vehicle to the spirit world. Rhythm is more than an idea or concept; it is the very foundation of building relations, spiritual as well as human. In this respect, rhythm and vibration (sound) are twins, and they complement each other very well.

There are four main forms of rhythms. They all behave differently, but they have similar results in terms of providing potential gateways to the world of spirit. The four forms of rhythm are:

- The rhythm of the spoken word
- The rhythm of dance (movement)
- The rhythm of music
- The rhythm of the written word

The Rhythm of the Spoken Word

From the indigenous perspective, the spoken word possesses much greater power than the written word. This is because the spoken word more overtly manifests the power of rhythm amplified by the sound and breath (or *mumoh*). The spoken word is, in fact, *mumoh* transformed into sound. Therefore, *mumoh* is inherent in the spoken word.

As I've said before, *mumoh* in the language of the Ga people means both breath and spirit. The elders teach that *mumoh* is the source of all speech. Because spirit manifests through breath, the most expedient medium for evoking spirit is the spoken word, according to my African wisdom. This is why all invocations and pouring of libations are performed with the spoken word in my culture. As I described in the previous chapter, the spoken word is given birth through a process of air passing through the vocal cords.

Eating in Silence

In the Ga culture, we are very sensitive to the power of speech; this also means we are attuned to the power of silence. When I was a little boy, I remember that my mother would be very troubled when we children would eat and speak at the same time. Again and again she would explain that the words that come out of our mouth are sacred, and that eating is a nourishing ritual. It is a waste of our sacred resources to be eating and talking at the same time. Furthermore, to benefit from a natural digestion of what we have eaten requires that we pay attention to the ritual of nourishment, that we truly *take in* what we are eating. This means that we should not talk while we eat but instead focus on the rhythm of chewing our food properly. Eating in my culture, then, is always done in silence. In the West, however, talking while eating is one of the main ways people socialize.

You might want to experiment with this idea in the following simple exercise.

PRACTICE TO UNLEASH THE HUMAN SPIRIT
EATING IN SILENCE

1. Invite a friend to dinner, and let him or her know beforehand that you will both be eating in silence.

2. Once the dinner is served, sit directly across from your friend, and eat without talking. Eat slowly, and listen to the dancing of the forks and knives and everything else, especially the sound and the rhythms that are created by both of you as you chew and swallow the food. It is very important to look at your friend in order not to miss anything. This is a lot of fun. Try it! And next time, invite several friends.

Call and Response

In African rituals, the people use a rhythm of call and response that is very powerful. The calls are punctuated with specific syncopation that assists in the creation of a sacred space. The elder, or *tsofa-tse* (pronounced *chofa-cheh*), initiates a loud call, which might be *"Tswa, tswa, omanye aba!"* (meaning "May prosperity be bestowed upon us!" or "May all our wishes be honored and brought to fruition!"). The people respond with a resounding cry of *"Hiao!"*

(pronounced *he-ah-oh*) (meaning "Let it be so! Let it manifest!"). The people who respond claim the gatekeeper role between this world and the spirit world.

To evoke spirit, the rhythm of the spoken word is employed by simply speaking the same phrases in repetition. Phrases repeated many times form a rhythmic circle, similar to the circle formed by repetitive beats on a drum. After a while, this brings about a hypnotic state of consciousness. The first level of awareness in this state of consciousness is a non-linear, non-reasoning state. Eventually, the speaker's whole being will be immersed into rhythmic space. This form of prayer is powerful because of the expedient vehicle the rhythm of the spoken word provides to teleport the speaker into the spirit world.

One example among the Ga people is the phrase *"Mi sumo bo!"* ("I love you!"), which a young man chants when he falls in love with a young woman:

> *Mi sumo bo!*
> *Mi sumo bo!*
> *Mi sumo bo!*
> *Mi sumo bo!*

I can tell you from personal experience that this is a very powerful and effective chant!

PRACTICE TO UNLEASH THE HUMAN SPIRIT
THE POWER OF REPETITIVE CHANTING

1. First, turn off your radio, TV, cell phone, beeper, and any other potential source of distraction. Sit quietly in a comfortable position.

2. Repeat the following chant, which means "Peace be with you!": *Hedzoleh aha bo! Hedzoleh aha bo! Hedzoleh aha bo! Hedzoleh aha bo! Hedzoleh aha bo! Hedzoleh aha bo! Hedzoleh aha bo!*

3. Repeat this chant for at least three minutes. For a truly profound experience, continue chanting for twenty minutes or more.

4. Chanting in a small group is even more powerful. This is a good way to start a group meditation, for example. There are many chants from traditions around the world that you can also experiment with. Enjoy!

The Rhythm of Dance (Movement)

No one really knows when humans started to dance. I would imagine that we have been dancing for as long as we have walked on this earth! For the Ga people, dance is considered sacred and imbued with deep healing powers. Because of this, my people believe all humans must dance.

The Ga people dance on all sorts of occasions. There are dances strictly for young women, such as the *Adowa* or the *Otofo,* which are puberty rite dances for teenage girls. This dancing takes place at the culmination of the rites marking their passage into womanhood. Some of these dances demand rigorous movement of the hands and feet, and on occasion of the pelvic region.

Dance speaks of beauty and of sensual power, and it is in all of us. Dance is a form of praying with our bodies. It is sacred! Yes, all dance is sacred! Some religions, in an effort to suppress people, have decreed that dancing should be forbidden. Since dancing fosters a freedom of bodily expression, by taking away this freedom religions reduce people to a level of subservience in order to try to control them. The powers-that-be fear that if people are allowed to dance, they will wake up their sacred selves! Then maybe they won't need these external authorities to mediate between them and the divine; they will experience the unleashing of the human spirit through their own means. Such an unleashing and awakening would create chaos with the hierarchy of organized religion, because in most churches, power is distributed in a vertical fashion, from the top down.

We cannot afford to give up our sacred right to dance. The myriad forms of dancing, from ballet to belly dancing, have but one purpose: to transport both audience and participants to a state of *mishe,* of happiness.

The contemporary theologian Matthew Fox has said, "Do not give a young person a doctorate degree without first teaching him or her how to dance!" I believe Dr. Fox is talking about cosmic dance. Cosmic dance involves more than bodily movement; it demands that dancers understand why they are dancing. Just as it is an awesome responsibility to hand a gun to people who lack the understanding that they possess a weapon, so it is with dance. Dancing is a powerful tool which enables a cosmic dancer to know the valleys of life, and on occasion to go to the mountaintop.

The rhythm of movement involves geometric wisdom. Dance usually requires music as a stimulant in order to evoke spirit. In Africa, the voice of the drum dictates the movement of the dancers, although it is possible to dance to the hidden music that surrounds us at all times. One day I saw a dance called "When Drums Were Forbidden." The dancers were dancing without music. It was a very eerie experience. The dancers had to count and measure in geometric calculations all of the departures and arrivals in order to synchronize their movements. This form of dance is easier to do when one person is doing the dance. Tap dancing is an exception, however, and it is an art form that can be executed easily with or without another source of music, because the rhythm of the tapping of the foot supplies all the music that is needed.

When dancer and dance become one, a state of *mishe* is born. Give yourself a taste of this experience through the following simple exercise.

Practice to Unleash the Human Spirit
Mindful Steps for Dancing to *Mishe*

1. Stand with your feet open two feet apart.

2. Sway with your entire body from right to left, and then from left to right. Repeat this several times.

3. Change your movement into a dance by gradually lifting your left foot and then your right foot an inch off the floor as you

sway. Continue this movement and feel a gentle wind caress your body as you dance yourself into a trance.

Rhythmic Sound

Rhythmic sound is the sound of music, and includes all the kinds of music we hear on the radio, on television, in movies, or produced by an orchestra or a choir. Every melody we listen to has rhythm. The rhythm of the melodic structure makes the song. In other words, without the rhythm, there would be no melody.

In rhythmic mutation, a musical note is changed to create a new rhythm by adding or lowering the value. For example, increasing the value of a quarter note to a half note, or lowering the value of a quarter note to an eighth note, alters the rhythm. Rhythmic mutation can also occur when the tempo of a musical phrase is changed from slow to fast, or from fast to slow. Rhythmic mutation is a process in which one rhythm gives birth to another.

When we are practicing mindful drumming, the degree of acceleration of the rhythmic phrase alters the emotional current experienced by the player or players. Mutation offers the opportunity to access and execute the diverse rhythmic information, creating a rich and varied experience. Rhythmic permutation rearranges a given musical phrase to create different effects. This offers an ocean of possibilities of sound combined with rhythmic mutation. In African fetish music, rhythmic mutation and permutation are fundamental and cause dancers to dance into the deep altered states of trance. The polyrhythmic mutations help create the circles of sound and energy that offer such an expedient vehicle to the state of *mishe*, or happiness.

PRACTICE TO UNLEASH THE HUMAN SPIRIT
EXPERIENCING DIVERSE POLYRHYTHMS

1. Once again, turn off your radio, TV, cell phone, beeper, and any other potential source of distraction. Get out your drum, or if

you don't have a drum, imagine your thighs to be a drum, or perhaps use your kitchen table. Sit quietly in a comfortable position.

2. Slowly start by playing half notes on your drum. As you place your right hand on the drum, count one and two. Then place your left hand on the drum and count three and four. Play this rhythm for at least three minutes.

3. Change the rhythm you're playing to quarter notes, by playing and counting the notes one, two, and then allowing your left hand to play the three, four notes. In other words, play beats one and two with your right hand, and beats three and four with your left hand. Play this rhythm at medium speed for at least three minutes.

4. Repeat steps 2 and 3, alternating the tempo until you feel comfortable with these two rhythms. Then change the speed, increasing it from moderate to fast. Notice the difference as you play the various speeds—slow, moderate, and fast.

5. For other examples, of mindful drumming rhythms, see Appendix C, and allow yourself to experiment!

The Rhythm of the Written Word

The written words in any language contains its own unique rhythm. This rhythmic essence gives the language motion or fluidity. The history of the written word dates back thousands of years. The rhythmic spirit of the written word means it continues to evolve.

In the chapter on the wisdom of the Ga people, I noted that on occasion the meaning and essence of a language is somewhat diminished when it is written. As such, there are languages that translate differently when they are written as opposed to spoken. The spoken language remains a more certain and direct path to the realm of spirit.

Nevertheless, the written word has its place, and it has allowed for the creation of many of the great gifts of culture, from the works of Shakespeare to the creative imaginings of novelists and short-story writers to the modern-day poetry of contemporary slam poets.

One of the most basic uses of the written word is in the realm of legal agreements and litigation. In the creation of agreement between two or more parties, the spirit of the written word has become a universally acceptable medium, and helps to cut down on misunderstanding and misinterpretation.

With all its limitations, the written words is still capable of invoking spiritual elements. Again, consider the great poetry and prose of human culture, which has allowed us to share a kinship with fellow humans across the centuries and across the oceans. The myriad mediums through which the written word can transport us into a state of *mishe* include poetry, plays, novels, and love letters, to name but a few.

The written word can trigger sad or happy emotions that can bring about deep healing. When you are reading a story and visualizing the images described in the story as a vehicle to transport you into the land of dreams and imagination, the door opens to the realm of the spirit world, where unlimited possibilities await. When you read a poem or a profound story, the message is generally filtered through a cognitive process for analysis. Then the heart decides if there is indeed information that provides spiritual inspiration and so merits integration. Given this two-level process, it is possible to read a poem or a story and experience a different emotional response depending on the transparency of your emotional fabric at the moment you're reading the story.

In America, I often see billboards with phrases such as "Be all you can be," or "Hunger hurts," or "America is at its best when catastrophe strikes." Taken in at a deep level, any of these phrases can catch our attention and on occasion arrest our imagination.

PRACTICE TO UNLEASH THE HUMAN SPIRIT
EXPERIENCING THE POWER OF THE WRITTEN WORD

1. Please read the following poem four times at a slower pace, and then read it at a moderate tempo:

Little Miss Muffett
Sat on a tuffet
Eating her curds and whey
Along came a spider
Who sat down beside her
And frightened Miss Muffet away

2. Repeat this process with following saying from the Ga people:

Kaamu efon! Smell no evil!
Kaanu efon! Hear no evil!
Kaana efon! See no evil!
Kaa susu efon! Think no evil!

3. What do you notice as you repeat these two poems? Now see how the following poem by Maya Angelou resonates:

Listening winds
Overhear my privacies
Spoken aloud (in your absence, but for your sake).

4. Now take a few minutes to write your own free-form poem of six to eight lines. Don't worry about rhyme or meter, but once you've expressed yourself, read what you've written four times, and see how the rhythm affects you, first at a slow tempo, and then at a quicker one.

The Awesome Power of Rhythm

In the course of this chapter, you've had a chance to experience a variety of different modalities for conveying rhythm. Please continue your experiments with rhythm as you go about your daily life. You will find that starting to pay attention to the awesome power of rhythm will give you the capacity to shift any of the so-called negative emotional states in the direction of *mishe* and *hedzoleh,* of happiness and peace.

Take the next couple of pages to write notes of your experience or draw pictures.

Mindful Drumming

NOTES

Chapter Six

Community Building in the Modern World

Community is the spirit,
the guiding light of the tribe,
whereby people come together
to fulfill a specific purpose,
to help others fulfill their purpose,
and to take care of one another.
Community is the grounding place
where people share their gifts
and receive from others.

~ Sobonfu Somé
Welcoming Spirit Home

Unleashing the Human Spirit

The timeless wisdom of my people teaches that we cannot find true happiness and peace in isolation. Unleashing the human spirit always involves, on some level, inclusion of our family, friends, and the larger community. Contemporary scientist and writer Brian Swimme eloquently expresses these fundamentals of African indigenous wisdom:

Isolation and alienation are profoundly false states of mind. We are born out of the Earth Community and its creativity and delight and adventure. Our natural state is intimacy within the encompassing community. Our natural genetic inheritance presents us with the possibility of forming deeply bonded relationships throughout all ten million species of life as well as throughout the nonliving component of the universe. Any ultimate separation from this larger and enveloping community is impossible, and any ideology that proposes that the universe is nothing but a collection of pre-consumer items is going to be maintained only at a terrible price.

As I pointed out in the very first chapter, one of the biggest benefits of mindful drumming is that it facilitates community building. The ongoing process of a group of people coming together to drum with the intention of evoking *mishe ke sumo* (happiness and love) is the essence of mindful drumming.

Community Spirit

Community spirit is a potent catalytic element that inspires love and happiness, trust and respect, self-esteem and high morale, caring and sharing, compassion, and a deep sense of ecumenism (that is, appreciation of the wisdom available from diverse sources). The characteristics of community spirit brought about by drumming in a group include:

Commitment: Commitment involves devoting your entire being to kinship with the community, which also means eternal connectedness. Commitment entails dedication, loyalty, and devotion to the vision and goals of the community. It reflects total awareness of the tenet of reciprocity—the truth that giving and receiving are the same. An alignment between your personal mission as an individual and the mission of the community is essential for community spirit to flourish.

Trust: Trust means relying upon and having confidence in the good that the community does and in the good that you do. It means knowing that there is a sense of fairness in the community.

Increased communication is evidence that members of the community are relying on one another. You know that the community offers good care to you and that you extend that same kindly care to all. Trust is the experience of a relationship of confidence between you and the community.

Love and Happiness: Community spirit always entails a sense of shared love and happiness. This includes knowing that love is the currency the community uses on all levels. Each moment, you experience the willingness to do your part to actualize that love. An alignment of happy feeling with intent, belief, and point of view, coupled with corresponding action in the world, allows you to experience that the entire community is working together for the success of the whole. You experience joy in all that you do that increases the effectiveness of the community. You work and smile at the same time, knowing that what you do brings joy to the hearts and minds of the people you serve and the people who serve you. You have an innate sense that service is play.

Ownership: Community spirit expresses the art of knowing that true ownership equals stewardship—being able to give all. You know that you are doing the work of community building, and you feel good about it. Taking ownership of your part in this deepens your knowing that you are contributing toward a greater good for future generations.

Authentic Power: Community spirit increases the ability to tap into the pool of unlimited, innate energy and the collective mind that unleashes the human will so that we can achieve our full potential. Authentic power allows you to feel the unlimited love that brought the human will into being. This power relies upon an eternal connectedness to the ancestors. Authentic power is the will that Jesus spoke about when describing the faith of a mustard seed and the ability to move mountains. There is an innate power living in all of us that often goes unrecognized; community spirit can awaken this power in you.

Courage: Courage entails personal resoluteness in the face of occasional failure, along with an ability to support each community member no matter what s/he is facing. Courage is the substance that we are made of, and gives us the ability to take risks for the larger good of the community and self. We may start out feeling afraid, but as we act with courage, we reach a sense of fearlessness that takes the community to greater heights.

Ecumenism: Ecumenism entails a deep respect for the diversity of human experience and wisdom. A sense of ecumenism arises mystically out of the community experience of rhythmic medicine. We overcome our differences when we drum together.

All of these characteristics of community spirit are inspired by the innate wisdom and facilitated by the act of drumming together. They are made manifest through the marriage of rhythm and sound.

We Are All Heroes

There are a number of significant examples of community spirit in the modern world, including the heroic acts of selfless sacrifice and love that took place after the terrorist attacks of September 11, 2001. The tragic events of September 11, as terrible as they were, also demonstrated the incredible power of the human spirit. In New York ordinary people demonstrated extraordinary heroism as they did what they could to help others. The cell phone calls made from the World Trade Center towers and the hijacked flight which crashed in the fields of Pennsylvania also reflected great courage and love. At the crucial moment, ordinary people facing the likelihood of imminent death did not speak of revenge or hatred; they spoke of their love for their families, and they wished them well before saying good-bye. Then they acted courageously according to the needs of the moment.

This loving instinct and potential for courage is in all of us. We were born with it. We only need to find access to it. Sometimes extraordinary moments bring this innate courage and love to the surface, as happened following the terrorist attacks. But we can also learn to cultivate this courage and love on a day-to-day level through mindful drumming.

A more mundane example of community spirit is reflected in many team sports. It is impossible to imagine Michael Jordan and the Chicago Bulls weaving their magic in winning the NBA championship without team spirit, which is simply community spirit in a specific guise. As all the players accept, uphold, and claim ownership of the vision of victory, it is then translated into action through community spirit. The honor and pride of a champion is to be a channel for the spirit of the combined inspiration and motivation of all the players, who also manifest the team spirit.

Just as mindful drumming brings the community together through a process similar to osmosis, the champion weaves the same magic on everyone around. The champion, by exhibiting commitment, a winning attitude, trust, ownership, happiness, authentic power, and unfaltering confidence, deciphers the community or team vision, triggering inspiration in his or her fellow team members. Everyone gets the message that there is only one option, and that is to win together.

In today's uncertain world, we all need community spirit. Families need community spirit. Individuals need community spirit. And the very planet we live on needs our community spirit! Mindful drumming provides one of the most effective ways for us to actualize the vision of a world that is truly a community. To inspire love and happiness, trust and respect, self-esteem and high morale, caring and sharing, compassion, and a deep sense of ecumenism, practice mindful drumming.

We are all potential champions. We are all potential heroes.

Through Western Eyes: Words from Dr. Dennis Hill
Building Intentional Community

Even before I met Kokomon, I had begun to listen to the indigenous wisdom of the African people. In 1995, my wife and I found out about a year-long mentorship training program in the cultural and spiritual ways of a remote tribal village in Burkina Faso, West Africa. The teachers were Sobonfu and Malidoma Somé of the Dagara tribe, who lived here in Oakland at the time. We completed the

program with thirty-five other people in the spring of 1996, and went through a two-day initiation under their supervision in a remote area of northern California.

By working and playing together over the course of a year, a true feeling of community developed among us; we became a bit of an extended village, even though we don't all live in the same place. Although some of the members have gone their separate ways since then, a core group of about twenty of us still gather monthly, rotating the meeting place among the members' homes. We still stay in touch over six years later, and we have learned a great deal about the value of community for our individual and collective health by direct experience over the years. We call ourselves, simply, "the village."

During that time, there have been three marriages, three new children, and one death in our group. We have known joy and sadness, peace and conflict, and the full range of human experience in our gatherings. We seem to have retained some kind of village cultural value, because we have been there for one another now over many years, and we still meet regularly even though we live miles apart.

Although our African teachers said they were not drummers, they did play the drum, as did many of the members of their African village. I bought my first djembe drum from them, and learned my first African rhythms. Throughout the year-long training, I saw and experienced the power of the drum to call people, to draw us in, and to unite us into a harmonious collective of human beings. I began to understand the meaning of creating, and holding, "rhythmic space." It was extraordinarily powerful.

To this day, all of our village gatherings begin with drumming. This has been our common theme throughout the years. The drums create a rhythmic space where each of us is a participant. We each participate in creating music together, with drums, shakers, and other rhythmic instruments. We sing and dance together. It is a group activity that includes everyone. Once we have taken the time to do this, we feel connected to one another and in rhythm, even if we haven't seen one another in a month or more. We can easily move from this space into other activities with a feeling of unity and oneness.

Ritual and Community Support

A little over a year ago, one of our village members told us she was about to go overseas to teach in Egypt for two years. She had been an active member of our village group, and now she was going to go away for a long period of time. The month before she was to leave, we gathered in our usual way, but in addition we heard her story about why she was making this bold career move.

After that, in a simple ritual, each of the village members offered a bead for a necklace that we created for her to wear while she was in Egypt so that she could remember her village group here at home, and know that we loved her and had not forgotten her.

We have made necklaces or bracelets for other members who have gone on trips overseas, and all have reported that they were comforted by knowing that it came from villagers here at home. The necklace or bracelet provided a tangible object connecting them to home while they were in a faraway place. This is just one example of how a ritual on the part of the community can be very empowering for the individual.

Since our friend needed help packing and cleaning out her house in preparation for her trip to Egypt the following month, we as a village decided to change our meeting location to her home in Grass Valley in northern California so that we could offer help in some way while we were there. She had specific tasks she needed done, and each of us pitched in to get them done for her. She was very appreciative of all our efforts on her behalf, but on the deepest level, each of us benefited from our participation, in that we got the tasks done in a communal way, and we were all working side by side for a common purpose. We were all in it together, helping one of our own.

Welcoming Ritual

Another ritual that we performed that same weekend involved a couple in our village who had just become parents of a new baby girl, their first child. She was just a tiny newborn, but they wanted to introduce her to the village members. None of us had met her yet.

According to the traditional view we had been taught during our mentorship, this baby is an ancestor who is making an appearance "on this side" for a specific purpose. She is a beautiful baby, and her parents are naturally quite proud of her.

Spontaneously, we came up with a ritual to welcome her. We had the parents and baby sit on the floor in the center of the village circle. Then each of the villagers began chanting or toning the baby's name, Leilani, in a polyrhythmic, overtoning, beautiful, and touching river of sound that immersed the three of them.

Although she was young, Leilani was clearly enjoying the sound and the attention. And of course each of the villagers enjoyed seeing the joy that we saw in her! Everyone benefited from this simple ritual.

It is worth noting that our village gatherings now include the children of the villagers on a regular basis, with ages ranging from teenagers down to the newborn. It wasn't always this way. When we started our training as a ritual village seven years ago, we were a group of adult strangers with our own personal emotional baggage and a measure of resistance to sharing our personal lives with other people. But as we have learned about a different way, the ancient way of communal living, we have grown to trust one another. We have come to a place where it is natural to extend ourselves to be involved and help fellow villagers as the need arises. Over the years we have evolved as a collective and as individuals, so that now it is a healthy place for children to be. We no longer need many hours just to figure out how to get along with one another! Issues may arise, but now we know how to deal with them. Our village children instinctively know that it is safe.

We have built an intentional community, and the key to it all has been the unifying effect and power of the drum.

The Creative Power of Community

When mindful drumming awakens us, we can move beyond our personal goals to the place of community where we can begin to identify the challenges in the community that need to be addressed.

Mindful drumming can help the community resolve specific problems. Such challenges could include overcoming domestic violence, reducing child truancy, or creating voting systems that encourage fairness, honesty, and inclusion—and operate from the understanding that the voice of the people is the voice of spirit.

To give one example, let us say that the challenge in our particular community is crime. We could create a drumming circle where everyone's intention and focus would be on what we could do to prevent crime. The rhythms and vibration of our drumming would first unite everyone present, and then allow us all to unite with *Nyogboh,* or Spirit, the cosmic creative force. The collective energy field or level of consciousness we would reach as a community would allow us to be open to discovering solutions in our quest to eradicate the problem of crime.

For illustration, perhaps we would be inspired to invite more young people to join our drumming circle. Or perhaps we would respond to the problem of crime in our community by deciding to get involved in one of the organizations that encourage interchange between youth and those we Americans call seniors—and my Ga people call elders. If hundreds of drumming circles focused on this problem of crime, what a difference this would make!

At our Attitudinal Healing Connection center in West Oakland, our mindful drumming has served to inspire us to offer ArtEsteem classes for community children, helping them develop the positive self-image and healthy self-regard that will inoculate them from using their energy in unproductive, negative ways (see Appendix D for more information on ArtEsteem). We sincerely do not want our children behind bars; therefore, we do our utmost to educate them. Ultimately, we want our children to participate in the cosmic dance of creation—to be fully human and to continue the creation story.

In my African culture, the concept of prison was an alien idea before the British colonized Ghana. However, even prisons can become true soul-processing facilities and foster real education if they are administered according to the principles of mindful drumming.

Mindful drumming creates the rhythmic space for us to come together and recognize our oneness. When we come to this recognition, we can only want for one another what we want for ourselves. Our priority becomes prosperity and love and justice, not just for the few, but for all. The principles and practice of mindful drumming can help us find the courage and the determination to bring this all to pass.

The Nigerian Nobel Prize–winning author Wole Soyinka offered a moving account of the power of community spirit in overcoming social problems on the occasion of the hundred-year anniversary of Emancipation in Trinidad and Tobago in his book entitled *The Burden of Memory, the Muse of Forgiveness.*

According to Soyinka:

The sunshine island of Trinidad, at last, decided that she was entitled to a place in postmodern history by staging her own coup d'état! In the uncertain atmosphere that followed this coup, some Trinidadians went on a looting spree. The shopping centers were mostly left untouched, for few were willing to venture that far from the security of their homes. No, it was the neighborhood stores that were broken into and looted. This is what shocked the majority of Trinidadians the most.

Taking advantage of the independent radio station that had escaped seizure, the chief of police went on the air and lectured the Trinidadians on their evil ways. Like a stern schoolmaster, he reminded them that this kind of act was un-Trinidadian and warned that it would not be tolerated. Then he gave them all forty-eight hours to return the looted property. "Just lay down your loot in front of your houses," he said. "We will come round and collect them, and return them to their owners. No questions asked. Return your loot, and let Trinidad return to herself." I drove around afterward with a friend. I could hardly believe my eyes. These goods were laid down neatly in front of the houses.

This is another example of calling upon community spirit to encourage people to act in harmony with the practices of the beloved community.

Spirits in Human Form

My people believe that we are all spirits in human form. Consider airplanes; one 747 jumbo jet carries over seven hundred passengers! If we stop and think for a moment, this is like taking a high-rise apartment building with seven hundred residents and transporting it through the sky. When we begin to think in terms of community, we can see that it is not just one little airplane flying from the United States to Ghana, for example, but seven hundred people—a whole village!—flying together. Who but spirits could come up with such a creation?

Similarly, a community with the single intention of using the technology of mindful drumming to invoke *mishe* and arrive at the doorstep of spirit, can transport us all to unleash our human spirit, or *mumoh*. This is truly a noble goal.

The Architecture of Community

We need to take a good hard look at what we as spirits in human form are creating together. Consider, for example, the modern high-rise. Recently I attended a lecture about architecture in the twenty-first century. The speaker pointed out that forty, fifty, and sixty years ago, the idea of the high-rise was conceived because of the cost of land. The high-rise, it was argued, would use space more effectively. This was the original ideal that led to the creation of the high-rise.

However, now architects are looking at community in the truest sense and noticing that the planning of high-rise buildings does not include the idea of people residing where they work. Instead, the high-rise building has been like a pump that people enter at the beginning of the day to do their work and then are pumped out at the end of the day. And since many people live fifty miles from where they work, every day they have to drive one hundred miles roundtrip. This whole concept is not working too well, particularly with expanding population growth and traffic congestion. Perhaps the high-rise in its current form is no longer the wisest use of land and resources.

If we think about community building for the next century and the next millennium, we would be wise to factor into our planning ideas such as people living and working in the same general area, perhaps even in the same building. Perhaps we can design our buildings with the true intention of community, so people can live within walking distance of where they work and where their children go to school, and in this way people won't have to drive so much, giving them more time for human interaction as well as preserving the environment.

Mindful drumming reminds us of who we are as people, first of all on the individual level, and then on the level of our connectedness to our brothers and sisters—that is, to the community. We need to look at the future and think of our intentions and goals from the perspective of coming together to break bread and find fellowship together. It shouldn't be necessary to drive fifty miles to be able to do that!

When we talk about the new communities that we want to build or the role that mindful drumming and creating a rhythmic space can play in the next millennium in reviving our inner cities, we need to remember that rhythm and sound bring people together and assist people in setting aside their differences, honoring their diversity, and celebrating their oneness. This is not something we need to invent! We can simply learn once again to tap into the timeless wisdom and harvest the awesome information that is available through mindful drumming.

Rebuilding Our Communities

Our greatest challenge in the next millennium is not likely to be space aliens coming to take over the Earth and kill us. There is no greater challenge or danger facing us today than the breakdown of our families and the breakdown of our communities, not just in the United States, but in the world community. This breakdown sows the seeds of violence and crime, and even helps to explain the roots of terrorism.

We need to return to the village concept. We need to go back and remember that rhythm and vibration are a common denominator we all can experience. It is from this place that we will be able to unleash the human spirit and solve the great problems that confront us, including war, hunger, crime, and the destruction of the environment.

On a collective level, time and again, I have heard participants in mindful drumming circles speak of their experience of connection. When mindful drumming is administered correctly in a community setting, people invariably experience kinship, even with people they didn't know—people they have just met for the first time.

Creating Mindful Drumming Circles

It is my deepest hope that once you have read this book and have experienced some of the many benefits of mindful drumming by practicing the exercises in the preceding chapters, you will be inspired to experience the incredible power of drumming in a community setting as well.

To that end, the following section provides detailed guidance for you in calling together a mindful drumming circle.

The Seven Principles of Mindful Drumming

1. One Heartbeat: The drum is the heartbeat of humanity, the ancestor of communication, and the pathway to the authentic soul of all beings. Whenever we drum mindfully, we raise our consciousness and connect with the oneness of humanity.

2. Universal Sister/Brotherhood: We recognize that all of humanity is related. We are all sisters and brothers. We are one.

3. Breath of Peace: When we hold an intention of peace as we breathe, we automatically awaken compassion and the spirit of peace. We listen and breathe deeply while we drum the rhythms of life. Breath is ritual.

4. Contagious Happiness: We are happiness. Happiness is our natural inheritance. When two or more of us join in silence, sound, and vibration, happiness is increased.

5. Infectious Joy: The spirit of joy lies in the twin concepts of rhythm and sound. Let us drum for the ancestors and receive the gift of joy, which provides a natural immunity to fear, pain, and suffering.

6. Creation of the Beloved Community: When hearts and minds are attuned to love, peace, and harmony, the beloved community is created. The beloved community reminds us of our oneness and enables us to practice ancient sacred rituals of deep ecumenism.

7. Service and Benevolence: Inspiration and openheartedness encourage us to give, to receive, and to reconnect with the source of our own rhythm. Service grounds us in the wisdom of surrendering to love.

How to Host a Mindful Drumming Meditation

If you are thinking of hosting a mindful drumming meditation, it is important to be aware of the power of the circle. Whenever two or more are joined with one intention, God is there, and the power of transformation is present. Mindful drumming meditation connects us with the pulse that unites us in mind, body, and spirit. Therefore, be aware that your decision to host a meditation is sacred, because whenever you join with others, you are creating community with spirit. Drumming together in unison is the quickest way to connect one human to another. It inspires cooperation and helps to create a beloved community. Hosting a mindful drumming meditation can be an inspiring and awesome experience.

Once you make the decision to host a mindful drumming meditation, you can use the following step-by-step guidance to ensure your experience is fruitful.

PRACTICE TO UNLEASH THE HUMAN SPIRIT
INSTRUCTIONS FOR MINDFUL DRUMMING CIRCLES

1. Make a list of the friends, relatives, co-workers, and associates you wish to invite to the mindful drumming meditation. Send out invitations by mail, telephone or e-mail to the people on your

list, or simply post flyers at your neighborhood center, community church, or grocery store.

2. As the initiating host, you will lead the first mindful drumming meditation. After the first meeting, if the group chooses to continue, you can decide whether to rotate the facilitation of the meditation.

3. I will refer to the facilitator of the mindful drumming meditation as the *circle leader*. For the sake of simplicity, the group can be called the *mindful drumming circle*.

4. When people arrive, have everyone sit comfortably in a circle, position their drums, and place their hands on their drums in silence. The circle makes it possible for everyone to see one another. Just being in a circle evokes the indigenous way of being together as equals. The circle creates immediate intimacy and kinship, which forms the matrix of a village. The circle also allows everyone the opportunity to lead and follow at the same time. The circle leader will encourage each member to look at the other group members' hands as the leader switches from rhythm to rhythm. This fosters a sense of interdependence and interconnections. What is within is also without.

5. Once everyone has arrived, people in the circle can give quick introductions (first names only). Keep the opening of the drumming circle as brief as possible. Leave all verbal exchanges or storytelling until the end of the drumming meditation. Silence is a very important space in the drumming meditation. The moments of silence are considered sacred.

6. The circle leader will sit in view of a clock for time-keeping purposes. The circle leader will open and close the circle as well as lead the circle through a series of drum rhythms. Each rhythm should be played for a duration of three minutes, at which point the circle leader will introduce a new rhythm.

7. The circle leader will give a brief explanation of mindful drumming meditation:

"Welcome to the circle! This is a mindful drumming meditation, and not a drumming jam session. The focus of the meditation is not on individual drumming expertise. The focus is on the community, and on the spirit and power of the community. Mindful drumming encourages participants to look at the whole and not at the fragments.

"In contrast to a drumming jam session, mindful drumming requires that everyone drum *in unison*, synchronizing rhythms and listening carefully to one another. This is made possible through following a group leader. The leader can be anyone—this time, I'm leading, but another time someone else might lead. The members of the circle are not in the circle to compete with one another or to go solo. The members of the circle are present to support one another and to play in unison together and to listen deeply to the sound of the vibrations and rhythms that emanate from the essence of the drum.

"Everyone is encouraged to look occasionally at their neighbors' hands while deeply listening to the sounds and playing the same rhythms as the circle leader. As the circle leader, I will play simple rhythms in 4/4 tempo or 3/4 tempo to avoid confusion.

"There must be no talking while drumming. Practice the art of deep listening. We'll be drumming for thirty minutes [for beginners] or one hour [for more advanced circles]. It is crucial that everyone stay throughout the process so that we can all experience the power of a mindful drumming meditation. If anyone needs to use the rest room, please do it now, before the meditation begins! [Allow a few minutes for this to happen, while the circle waits in silence.]

"To avoid disruptive noises and distractions during the drumming meditation, please take off your watches and turn off all electronic equipment, such as cell phones, beepers, and timers on watches. During the meditation, there will be uninterrupted drumming and listening.

"It is important to remember that in mindful drumming we do not *beat* the drum, or the drum will beat us! *We communicate with the drum!* The drum is the heartbeat of humanity. If you just tap lightly, you will hear the sounds that emanate from the various parts of the skin of the drum. Remember that this was once a living and breathing being—the skin of the drum came from a deer or goat, and the wood came from a tree. These beings gave themselves to you so you could have this experience. So treat the drum as sacred.

"While you're drumming, if you feel tired, just take a rest for a while by allowing your hands to open wide with your palms flat on the skin of the drum, with the drum tilted slightly. You will feel the vibrations of all the other drums flowing through your drum into your hands, so you will still be communing with the other mindful drummers. As everyone plays in unison, you will experience the love essence of the beloved community. When you feel rested, rejoin the drumming. It will feel as if you have never left. Now, let us begin."

8. At this time, the circle leader will guide the group through a series of polyrhythms in 4/4 or 3/4 tempo, maintaining each rhythm for three or four minutes, and then switching to another rhythm for three or four minutes, and so on until the half-hour or hour has passed.

[*Tips for first-time leaders:* Remember there is no need to make this complicated! The secret is everyone playing in unison, using beats of equal duration. Start with a very simple rhythm; for example, play beat one with your right hand, and beat two with your left, beat three with your right hand, and four with your left while watching and listening to the group. Then, after three or four minutes, change the rhythm by playing beats one and two with your right hand and beats three and four with your left hand. Also, experiment with creating natural sounds like wind or the ocean or rain. Yes! You can create these sounds on your drum by gently rotating your hands on the animal skin to create wind or the ocean, and by resting your fingers on the skin and gradually lifting one

finger at a time to create rain. To create rain, first move your fingers slowly, then increase the speed to medium beat. Listen carefully to the sounds as you start from the center of the drum and gradually move to the edge and experience the range of rain energy as it emerges. It's fun!]

9. As the end of the drumming time nears, the circle leader brings the drumming to a conclusion by lowering the volume gradually until everyone stops playing. When all drumming has ceased and the participants' hands are resting on the drums, the circle leader speaks: "Now, just let yourselves inhale slowly and exhale slowly, inhale slowly and exhale slowly, inhale slowly and exhale slowly, then rest for the next few moments."

10. Now is the time for the group members to check in or share in sacred storytelling. Depending on the size of the group, this can take from fifteen minutes to a half hour. Go around the circle one by one, and allow each person a few minutes to share what they experienced while they were drumming. Remind group members of the sacredness of the experience and the importance of listening deeply to one another in a spirit of mutual respect and confidentiality during this sharing period. Everyone's journey during the drumming will be unique and deserves respect.

11. In closing, the circle leader asks the group members to stand in a circle and hold hands while leading the chant: "This is an ancient gratitude call to the ancestors from the Ga language and traditions. I will say, '*Tswa, tswa, omanye aba!*' meaning 'May we be blessed! May all our wishes be granted and brought to fruition,' and the whole group will loudly proclaim, '*Hiao!*' (pronounced *he-ah-oh*), meaning 'May it be so! Let it manifest!' So: *Tswa, tswa, omanye aba!*"

12. Finally, the circle leader encourages everyone in the group to hug everyone else in parting.

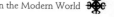

Mindful Drumming Meditation Synopsis

1. Invite people to circle.
2. Select a leader (usually the host for the first time).
3. Give introductions by calling out first names into the circle.
4. Give brief introduction to mindful drumming meditation.
5. Take a quick bathroom break; advise everyone to turn off all electronic equipment.
6. Set the length of time for the drumming (half an hour or an hour), and remind people not to talk while drumming.
7. Lead the circle through a series of polyrhythms, allowing three to four minutes for each rhythm.
8. End the drumming, by gradually lowering the volume.
9. Have everyone take three deep, slow breaths, inhaling and exhaling slowly.
10. Have each member of the circle share what came up for her/him during the drumming.
11. Stand in a circle holding hands while closing with the gratitude call to the ancestors.
12. Have everyone in the group hug everyone else in parting.

Community Building

There are as many ways to build community as the infinite human spirit can imagine! My people teach that we cannot be in any community by ourselves without relatedness to the ancestors. It is because of them that we are here. Therefore, in order to continue their legacy, we need to take the steps necessary to achieve a peaceful community of respectful coexistence.

Now is the only time there is, and each of us are called upon to make a concerted effort to apply the principles of community spirit for the sake of our friends and families and our future children for seven generations to come as we move into the next millennium. Following are some ideas on how you can go about building community where you live.

Practice to Unleash the Human Spirit
Ten Ways to Build Community

1. Referring to the instructions earlier in this chapter, host a one-time mindful drumming circle; then see if participants are interested in creating an ongoing circle on either a weekly or a monthly basis.

2. Host a monthly or seasonal event on the full moon or on the Solstice or Equinox, or on a holiday such as Martin Luther King Jr. Day, Earth Day, or Grandparents Day. Be sure to include people of all ages, including children and community elders.

(a) To host a monthly event such as a Full Moon celebration, invite friends, co-workers, acquaintances, or neighbors and have everyone bring a favorite food to share. Begin the gathering by asking everyone to sit in a circle. Sitting in a circle suggests a collective and communal approach. There are many kinds of Full Moon celebrations, but whatever type you decide upon, keep the format of a circle. A circle is powerful! Practicing fifteen to twenty minutes of silence is a wonderful ritual that raises the vibrations of the circle and helps to ground the participants in their divinity. At the end of the agreed-upon time of silence, open the discussion with a check-in and ask participants to share what brought them. You may also want to ask participants to comment on the wonder and awesome beauty and power of the full moon. Keep the meeting short—perhaps one and a half hours. Close with a sharing of food.

(b) For seasonal events, such as the Solstice or Equinox, follow the above instructions, but focus the intention on the uniqueness of the season.

(c) To organize an event such as a celebration for Martin Luther King Jr. Day, you'll need a committee of seven to twelve people to assist in planning. You'll need at least twelve months to plan a successful large event. This is a favorite holiday of ours, because it precedes and prepares us for the Season for Nonviolence, which begins January 30 and ends April 4. This gives time to get the community involved in ending violence. Dr. King's life was dedicated to ending fear, discrimination, and violence, and uplifting the poor of the world while educating all of us about the violence of poverty and injustice. You can ask your church or other community organization to join you in this effort, because such entities love to serve their communities and may have access to land or an appropriate location for the event. An important factor to remember in celebrating Martin Luther King Jr. Day is that you can get your entire community involved in service work. People have an inborn ability to serve, and joy and service are synonymous. We need to emulate King's life as well as celebrate it!

If you fuse the two celebrations together in some way—Martin Luther King Jr. Day and the Season for Nonviolence—you will be bringing together the lifework of two great human beings. The Season for Nonviolence commemorates the assassination of Mahatma Gandhi on January 30 and the assassination of Martin Luther King Jr. on April 4. There are sixty-four days in the Season for Nonviolence, and you are asking your community to join you and your friends in taking a vacation from violence for these sixty-four days. The beauty of the event is that it is both internal and external. You are asking your friends to join you in practicing what Gandhi said: "Be the change that you want to see." By sharing all of this with your friends who have joined you to form a committee to put on a special celebration, you are participating in what is called *self-development activism*. At the same time, you are sharing your passion with them, giving them tools to work on themselves, improving the lives of all members of the community, and celebrating the lives of great human beings.

Make sure your committee keeps in mind the following elements: a nonpolitical agenda (that is, a focus on spiritual or social consciousness raising), cost, need for fundraising (sell space to vendors, obtain grants, etc.), publicity, live music (invite a local band), and potential speakers (you might consider inviting a celebrity who feels passionately about King, such as Congresswoman Barbara Lee or actor Danny Glover).

(d) To organize an event such as Earth Day, you also need a

committee and advance lead time (see comments regarding Martin Luther King Jr. Day above). Many areas already have regular Earth Day celebrations, so you may choose to join a preexisting planning group, perhaps forming a subcommittee with some of your neighbors and friends. The focus will be on stewardship of the Earth, and possible speakers to invite include environmentalists such as activist Julia Butterfly Hill or actor/director Robert Redford.

3. Start a sports league for children, or volunteer your services at a league that already exists. You don't necessarily have to go through a school, but if you have the consent and support of a principal, you can reach more children, and parents may feel more comfortable. Remember, your primary intention is community building, so be sure to ask your friends and neighbors to join you in the planning and execution. If you wish to start a soccer junior league for girls and boys, you will need to create at least two teams to play each other. Each team will need uniforms, shoes, and soccer balls. You will also need volunteers to serve as referees and to help to govern the game. Contact senior citizen centers in your community, and let them know how crucial it is for them to be involved in the children's game, whether as coaches, judges, or spectators. For the creation of basketball or football leagues, again consider working with a school. And check with other junior leagues in the area to learn from their mistakes and successes.

4. Participate in a community garden. If there isn't one in your area, consider starting one! Because land in urban areas is scarce, I suggest you search for an existing community garden before you start from scratch. However, if there is no community garden in your area, or if existing gardens are full, contact a church in your area and propose to organize one. If you see an empty lot in your neighborhood, and it appears to be abandoned or neglected, call the city government to see if it's possible to obtain the blighted lot for community purposes. Because this can be a lengthy process, you may choose instead to contact your local school. Schools are

always in need of support from the community, and just as it takes a whole village to support a child, it takes a whole community to support a school! A garden on school grounds brings the usual benefits of gardens right to our children, including fostering their relationship with the earth, plants, insects, birds, and the environment. They also get to learn the scientific aspects of gardening, including biology and chemistry. You can't go wrong with this one! The children will learn firsthand where tomatoes and squash come from, and they'll be much more enthusiastic about eating fresh fruits and vegetables.

In building a community garden, you can contact lumber yards and nurseries for donations of soil, seeds, and plants. Once you've acquired the land and connected with various partners, organize a day of weeding, clearing, digging, and leveling the ground. Upon completion, set another day for creating planting boxes and composting areas. Ask your partnering nursery the best time to plant various kinds of seeds in your area, and plan a seasonal planting schedule. Then plan a planting day and invite your friends to help. Since this is a community garden, it is important that everyone participate in watering and nurturing the growing plants. Set schedules for watering, weeding, and other tasks so that it is convenient for everyone. Let the community reach consensus on the best plan. When flowers, vegetables, fruits, and herbs are ready for harvest, get together and discuss who to share with and talk about what seeds to plant for the next season. If you have more than you can eat yourselves, consider donating the extra produce to a local food bank to serve the wider community.

5. Organize rites of passage for the girls and boys in your family or larger community. These don't have to follow a particular form. Be creative!

(a) Rites of passage for adolescent girls are much needed. Such rites help build self-esteem and help them define their growth and development into young women. This will require female bonding. Get together with a few female friends and talk about what it was like growing up. Once your friends are open and receptive, ask them if they would be interested in mentoring some young women who are entering puberty. Topics could include entering into puberty, claiming power as women, and exploring the power of a woman's moon cycle. Both adult women and the young girls entering womanhood would get a lot of joy out of these gatherings. The adult women, including mothers, friends, and aunts of the teenage girls, would create ritual and focus sacred discussion on topics such as feminine wisdom, survival skills (gathering food, cooking, washing, cleaning, etc.), education, menstruation, beauty, sex and its consequences, right timing for bearing children, roles of women in the twenty-first century, women's history, the feminine face of God, Goddess energy, war and peace, work, and relationships, such as dating and marriage. Plan some rites of passage, and set seven days or two weeks for the girls to undergo these rites, followed by a completion ceremony. In my culture, the young women are dressed as princesses and the entire community comes out to honor them. You may elect to have a simpler ceremony. Again, be creative!

(b) Rites of passage for boys are organized and executed by men. Ask some of your male friends to create a course. For example, find a park or place to take the boys entering manhood to a camp. It is important to get them out of the inner city into a more natural setting, such as a campground, in order for them to be in nature. Consider focusing on some of the following topics: masculine wisdom, survival skills (gathering food, cooking, washing, cleaning, etc.), education, physical changes that come with puberty, compassion, learning to respect and honor their own feminine energy, war and peace, sex and its consequences, right timing for bearing children, work, and relationships, such as dating and marriage. After whatever rites of passage you have planned, end with a completion ceremony. Perhaps each young man can sing a song and create a dance. Once again, be creative! Find a visible way for the community to acknowledge these young men.

6. Host a dinner where you share food in silence (as in the earlier practice in Chapter Five), with one friend. Yes! Experiment with just one friend. Invite a friend to dinner, and explain to her/him that you want to share food without talking during the meal. Tell her/him that you respect her/his opinion and would like to know afterward what her/his experience was. When your friend arrives, again explain the ritual and get any petty talk out of the way before you sit at the table. Have all the food and drinks already waiting on the table. Turn any music off, along with all cellular phones or beepers. Ask your guest to do the same. Once you and your friend sit, quietly say, "We are grateful for this food as it nourishes our body and spirit." Then begin to eat in silence. Please eat as slowly as you can. Try to savor your food and give the chewing of each bite your full attention. When you have finished your meal, sit quietly for a moment. Then leave the table and go to another room, or clear the table completely, and hold a dialogue on what was going on in your hearts and minds while you ate.

Do this again with another friend until you are comfortable with the process, then invite more than one person. The more people who participate, the deeper and more profound the experience. You can host this Eating in Silence for breakfast or lunch, but I highly recommend dinner because then you need not rush the process. Be sure to allow sufficient time to enjoy the experience.

7. In today's world, there are so many elders who feel left out and unproductive. I believe that bringing them together with younger people is one of the most rewarding things we can do. Plan a field trip to a scientific laboratory, museum, zoo, baseball game, or park (to name only a few ideas). Decide upon a date, and plan your outing. Once you have a date, contact a school or boys or girls clubs, along with a senior center in your area, and extend the invitation. Invite at least one elder for every two children. If you are taking six children, you'll need three elders. Keep it simple and fun, and start small. On your first attempt, plan for half a day, then end with lunch before taking everyone home. This is so much fun! I hope you'll try it.

8. Build community through art. Dr. Matthew Fox has written in his book *Original Blessing*, "Art as meditation takes one on deeper, more communal journeys than words can ever do."

(a) Invite your friends and neighbors over to do a visioning of how to beautify or clean up a particular area of the community. Include a potluck as part of the event, and tell everyone to plan to spend about two hours on fun and play. You will need colored markers and 36 by 36-inch butcher paper. Sit in a large circle and ask everyone to visualize the area that they have chosen to clean up. Take ten to fifteen minutes of deep silence, followed by another ten to fifteen minutes of guided visualization. Imagine what you would like to see in your community. What would serve everyone, young and old, rich and poor, male and female, two-legged and four-legged? After these twenty to thirty minutes of silence and visioning, divide into smaller groups of two, three, or four people. Give each small group a sheet of butcher paper and colored markers and ask them to draw what came to them during their silent meditation. Give each group about thirty minutes to draw their experience, and then another thirty minutes to discuss their creations with the small group. Then have everyone assemble in the larger group to share what came up as you eat the food, drink, and make merry. (This art project may lead to follow-up plans to implement some of the creative ideas that emerge.)

(b) Call the community together to beautify a wall by creating a mural that reflects cross-cultural connections and inspires peaceful coexistence. This can be a small project or a large one, but whatever art project you decide to do as a community needs to focus on playing, having fun, and creating beauty together.

(c) Invite some friends and neighbors over, and give each person a piece of clay to sculpt. Ask them to create anything imaginable with their eyes closed.

(d) Invite your friends and neighbors over, and ask them to sit in a circle. Start a story, and go around the circle, having each person contribute a paragraph until the story is complete. Encourage the principles of sincerity and paying attention from the heart.

9. Organize or participate in an Earth stewardship club or organization in honor of Mother Earth. There are already organizations that are doing fantastic work, such as Tribe of Heart, which uses storytelling, visual media, and the arts to present a vision of a compassionate future, and EarthSave, an educational, social, and activist network with a very big heart, and Yes!, which educates, inspires, and empowers young people ages fifteen to thirty to embrace the wisdom of environmental sanity through its weeklong summer camps. I highly encourage joining these worthwhile organizations. For more information, see Appendix D.

If the focus is to organize a day and celebrate the feminine principle in honor of Mother Earth, it is important to allow women to be the catalyst and organizers of such an event. For example, my wife, Aeeshah, has shared with me that the Community Learning Department of the University of Creation Spirituality is organizing a gathering of women to plan an event to honor the Great Mother and celebrate the power of feminine energy in nature and the feminine face of God. In the African indigenous culture, the feminine and the masculine are equally important. We always begin our prayers to the Great Spirit by calling on Father/Mother God. Among the Ashanti people, the chief is chosen by the Queen Mother. The feminine balance in nature creates harmony. The feminine includes the qualities of compassion, patience, deep listening, and the art of nurturing. Organizing a day to honor Mother Earth provides the entire community with an awesome opportunity to witness and partake of the power of the feminine principle.

10. Joining an organization that brings people together to do some kind of physical activity on a regular basis is a great way to build community. There are many existing community groups you could consider joining, or you could create one of your own. It is also wonderful to volunteer with organizations that do AIDS education or other health-related organizations that plan yearly walk-a-thons, run-a-thons, or bike-a-thons. These are great community-building activities, and many times you have to prepare all year

long to be physically fit enough to handle such commitments. Join an organization or find some other way to get together regularly with a group of people and nurture your community spirit. Also explore the following possibilities.

(a) Join a community chorus. Singing is fun. Let your voice and spirit sing for joy!

(b) Join a bicycle club. If there is no such club and you love biking, consider starting one. Walking or hiking together on a regular basis is also a good way to foster community.

(c) Join a book club or start one, for reading and discussing books together. Or consider joining or creating a writing group.

(d) Join a square dancing club, or participate in some other form of dance. Again, if there isn't a club already, start one!

As we travel along our life path and attempt to engage deeply with our neighbors and build community, may we strive to be happy learners rather than destroy ourselves over petty issues. Being happy learners means finding that place within us that has the answers to our deepest questions and that can resolve even the most challenging problems. This is the place we can access through experiencing the twin realities of rhythm and sound, thereby unleashing our human spirit and enjoying the full fruits of the beloved community in harmony with ourselves and one another.

Take the next couple of pages to write notes of your experience or draw pictures.

NOTES

NOTES

Chapter Seven

Discovering Your Own Rhythm

Take a journey to rhythm-hood,
and find yourself.

~ Kokomon Clottey

Finding Your Own Rhythm

This chapter is about finding your own rhythm, your own path to the world of spirit. Finding your own true rhythm is analogous to what mythologist Joseph Campbell termed "following your bliss." People often think of following your bliss in terms of finding your true vocation or life's work. The discovery of your own rhythm, however, is even farther reaching. It is an essential step on the path to selfhood or self-actualization. It means finding the vehicle that best suits your essential being as you journey on the path to spirit.

Finding your own rhythm can be the first step on a journey whose destination is the journey itself. The process of discovering can be likened to peeling off layer after layer of an onion with millions of layers.

I have heard of many people in the West who spend many years educating themselves to practice in a particular field and then, some time after getting their license or degree and working for a while, become disenchanted and quit. The cost is enormous. To prevent this waste, it could prove helpful to search at an early age to discover our true vocation in relation to the cosmos, to find a way we can contribute that is in tune with natural principles. Once people find and uncover their innate rhythm, this naturally leads to an awakening to their true vocation.

Through Western Eyes: Words from Dr. Dennis Hill
Finding Our Own Rhythm

Finding our rhythm ultimately means experiencing our own life as individuals while also experiencing our own life as a member of the collective life, that is, as members of our own community. This is the powerful message I have received from Kokomon and other indigenous teachers. We are all human spirits, and together we form the whole of the human spirit. When we come from that place of knowing, differences recede. We are all human beings, and we are all capable of being humane.

This humane instinct is in everyone. The events of September 11, 2001, demonstrate this powerful instinct. At the crucial moment, ordinary people did extraordinary things and put themselves at risk to help other ordinary people, many of whom were complete strangers. Many lost their very lives helping others. This is a powerful testament to the existence of the human spirit. Our task, then, is to get in touch with this powerful source of courage, compassion, and wisdom.

Kokomon has offered his cultural method of mindful drumming meditation to us as a means to get to that great power source that resides with all of us. When we successfully get to that place through our rhythmic practice, we can experience our connection not only to other human beings but to all living beings.

Easy Steps to Discovering Your Rhythm

The very first step to discovering your own rhythm is to perform a self-diagnosis. This entails paying attention to what you really, truly enjoy. You can use the following exercise to help you in this process.

PRACTICE TO UNLEASH THE HUMAN SPIRIT
PERFORMING A SELF-DIAGNOSIS

1. Begin an honest appraisal of the activities you enjoy. For example, do you prefer drumming to dancing, or vice versa? Do you enjoy swimming, walking, or running? Do you love to paint or write? All of these activities are equally valid paths to the spirit world. Allow yourself to move beyond judgment and honestly explore what is really true for you. Remember, it is important not to compete with yourself or compare yourself with others.

2. You may wish to record your insights in a journal, which you can add to over time as new ideas come to you, perhaps while you're drumming.

3. Next, set aside a time and make a date with yourself to experience the activity or activities you most enjoy. Be mindful as you take yourself through the activity of your choice. Again, record your insights in your journal. As your experience unfolds, listen to your heart and record the wisdom it speaks to you.

4. Return to this exercise after some time has passed, perhaps after a week or a month have gone by. Feel free to keep practicing your desired activity. See how you feel about your favored activity from this vantage point of time going by.

Note: You can also help your children discover their life's path by guiding them through a similar process.

My people say that our senses function as canoes in which we can travel to the spirit world. There are thus five main vehicles of entry that make the journey possible: seeing, hearing, smelling, touching, tasting, and feeling. Again, it is important to know which medium to choose as a personal path. Thinking of this in terms of the preceding exercise, you can also consider whether you might choose to elect dancing over drumming, or chanting over dancing.

The intention is simply to find the way that makes the journey smooth, fun, and expedient *for you.*

Some people may find traveling by canoe to be smoother than riding on a horse. Others may choose to travel by airplane instead of by boat to cut down on time. All mediums are equally valid, but it is important for you to figure out what vehicle truly brings you joy. You can modify the practice of self-diagnosis to keep honing in on this. Of course, you may find that a combination of activities provides the right key for you: Perhaps you'll decide you like to practice some form of movement, such as tai chi or dancing before you drum or chant, for example.

Again, any of the senses can provide a vehicle for transporting you into trance, into an altered state of consciousness where you are in touch with spirit. The way to select your vehicle is to become as a child and let yourself experiment with a spirit of play. One of the beautiful things about children is that they're not afraid to try fun new games, even though they know that sometimes it means making a fool of themselves and maybe even getting hurt. Children are generally more willing to jump into the river and get wet!

Through Western Eyes: Words from Dr. Dennis Hill
Indigenous Virtual Reality

When we engage in mindful drumming, we sometimes find we feel the presence of ancient ancestors. I have shared how I have even heard voices singing. Others have reported experiencing a beautiful natural environment, or the presence of wild animals. This is a subjective experience, and everyone who tries this method will have his or her own experience. But the point is that through these experiences, our own lives expand to include all these other people and living beings. One could call this experience "indigenous virtual reality." Through mindful drumming, we can experience this virtual reality where we transcend the confines of time and space to commune with the ancestors and other beings in our life.

I remember attending an outdoor community celebration at Mosswood Park in Oakland called Carijama, a celebration of African and Caribbean music and culture. Many people had brought their own drums. Suddenly I noticed a toddler about a year and a half old. He was absolutely absorbed in playing a drum that was lying on the ground. He was playing with both hands and completely focused on the sound he was creating. I was mesmerized by the scene of this incredibly young person so engrossed in playing the drum.

Too soon, an adult joined him, attempting to show him how to play. The spell was broken. The child stopped playing. The impression I had was that the playing and sound were instinctive in that child, but as soon as he was interrupted, it was over, at least for the time being. But during the absorbed playing, I definitely had the image of the ancestral energy in that little boy. It was as if he brought that rhythmic ability forward into this life from his ancestral past.

Children have no preconceived notions about drumming, about race, about the wealth of their playmates' parents, or about their political persuasions. Children are children. And we are all former children. When we gather together to drum, we are gathering together to play as children. Innocent children have vivid imaginations. We all can remember when a childhood friend or family member walked through our imaginary fort or our imaginary farm or baby's room; this was all very real at the time. I remember a story about the noted scholar in the field of comparative mythology Joseph Campbell. He was visiting a colleague and parked his car in front of his colleague's house. But the colleague's little daughter was out playing house in the front yard and told Campbell that his car was blocking the front door of her house. Rather than dismiss the child, Campbell moved his car. He showed respect for the child's inner world. We need to learn to show the same kind of respect for ourselves!

Becoming a Child Again

Let us remember that our primary goal in finding our own rhythm is *mishe,* or happiness. Therefore, it is very important to know that this process is not about ego. Discovering one's rhythm and finding one's true vocation can be a very arduous journey for some people. Why is it difficult and challenging? I would say that it is because of the mind.

My friend John, who is an engineer, shared with me his desire to play in a band or an orchestra. But he thought this desire was impossible to fulfill. One day, however, he entered the sacred space of a mindful drumming circle. During the mindful drumming meditation, he experienced an incredible experience of *mishe*. This experience freed him up so that he realized there might be other ways he could experience his dream of creating beautiful sound and rhythm with others.

The point is simple. The mind is a trickster, and all too often can get in our way of seeing the obvious. We are wise to keep ego out of our decisions and instead exercise our choice and free will. Any decision we make can always be changed at a future date if we find that what we've chosen isn't working. After traversing many paths, we are finally ready to experiment with at least one vehicle. This is inevitable.

In my early years, I tried a variety of vehicles myself. I'll share one such encounter with you. I well remember my very first astral journey. It was one bumpy ride! There was a full moon in my African homeland. It was a warm peaceful night, with the sounds of the waves of the Atlantic Ocean punctuated by crickets in the background. I had been playing with my band at the Star Hotel that night. Afterward, I went outside, and I lay down to rest. Soon I felt myself being elevated, slowly at first, then with a sort of jumpy motion like a kangaroo, and finally with a sense of graduating into what seemed like a space walk.

Next I found myself in the air over and above some very big and tall balboa trees. At first, I was afraid. Then I started putting things into proper perspective. I had had my divination, and the time had come for me to take some baby steps into the spirit world. I had been told by Ghanaba, my godfather and spiritual teacher, to become a child. Only then would it be possible for me to experience the spirit world and fulfill my life's dream. I looked around myself with fresh eyes.

Declaring Sacred Space

Along with self-diagnosis to find what you truly enjoy and becoming like a child again, another way to facilitate our discovery of our own rhythm is by declaring sacred space. By this I mean consciously setting aside the time and space to practice our preferred activity, whether it be dancing, chanting, drumming, or painting, and allowing ourselves just to get in the rhythm of it. In this way, we can reach the place of timelessness where all answers dwell.

Through Western Eyes: Words from Dr. Dennis Hill

I will share with you a simple anecdote about how we can find moments of timelessness even amidst our busy lives here in the West. I've found that this is a crucial aspect of finding our own rhythm. Recently, while I was waiting for my wife to get out of the car in a crowded grocery store parking lot, my eyes were drawn to some beautiful green trees in the distance swaying in the breeze. Immediately adjacent to the swaying trees was the 580 freeway, and I could see the cars whizzing by and hear the low but constant roar of the freeway noise. Yet the swaying trees gave me a vivid reminder of the sacred rhythmic natural life of the trees, in juxtaposition to the fast pace we maintain in our modern urban environment. For a moment as I focused on the trees, time was suspended.

It occurred to me that through rituals creating sacred space, time is suspended intentionally. An ordinary place becomes a timeless place. Ideally events will unfold in a natural way with their own rhythm. Perhaps we have more of a choice than we've realized to declare sacred space for ourselves that is separate from the pressures and paces of our everyday world.

The Journey to Finding Your Own Rhythm

There are two basic ways to experience the journey to finding your own rhythm—passive or participatory. Both are valuable. Passive experience, for example, might entail looking at a painting or other piece of artwork by a great master, such as Picasso or Michelangelo. Attending a play, concert, movie, or musical show can also induce trance. Be open to whatever happens for you.

Participatory aspects of the journey to the spirit world include speaking, singing, drawing, dancing, or drumming ourselves into a state of *mishe*. The various exercises in this book describe participatory forms of transporting yourself to the realm of the ancestors.

On a recent visit to Kokrobite, in Ghana, West Africa, I had an experience of a journey to the spirit world that started out as passive experience but soon became participatory. I was attending a performance by the Royal Obonu Drummers. In the dark shadow of the new moon, seven black African men emerged with a *fron-ton-fron*. A *fron-ton-fron*, like its name, is an enormous ceremonial drum which stands five and a half feet high and weighs over one hundred pounds. A fat sound emanated from this drum that penetrated my soul like the scorching African sun in December. It exploded and released intense heat and loud sounds like thunder as the drummers beat it with great intensity.

This thunderous sound arrested my spirit and dragged me to the floor. Suddenly, I was dancing, and my temperature began to rise. My armpits immediately started breathing like my nose as it warmed. An ancient happy feeling began to arise in me. My ancestral spirits wrapped me in a kente, a traditional Ghanaian cloth, and lifted me higher and higher as the thunderous sounds of the *fron-ton-fron* faded. I was free at last. The experience transported me to when I was a child, carefree, laughing, and playing in the security of my community.

In this state, I experienced a deep love for my body, for myself, for my very being. The following exercise can help transport you to a similar love, if you let it.

Practice to Unleash the Human Spirit
Loving Your Body

1. Set aside some time for a leisurely and pleasurable shower or bath without interruptions. That means being sure to turn off the telephone and disconnect any beepers or cell phones that might otherwise disturb your space.

2. In the shower: As you stand naked in the shower, imagine you are standing on a magic carpet and sing a simple song to yourself, preferably a lullaby. It might be a song you remember from childhood, or, if you like, you can sing something simple like "Love my body, love my body." In my language, it goes, "*Sumo gbomotso, sumo gbomotso.*" As you listen to the sound of the falling water and the singing that emanates from the depths of your being, feel the water like drum beats caressing your skin.

3. In the tub: Sit naked in a tub of warm or hot water in a comfortable position. You might want to light a scented or unscented candle and set it nearby. You could also choose to put some scented essential oil in the water, such as lilac, frankincense, or sandalwood. Rest your hands on your solar plexus, just above your navel, and sing a lullaby or the simple words suggested above: "Love my body, love my body" or "*Sumo gbomotso, sumo gbomotso.*" As you sing, feel the sound emanating from your center, and observe how the water vibrates as you sing.

4. Listen and feel the sounds of the rhythm of the water, and the sounds of the rhythm of your own voice, and allow yourself to be transported to the spirit world. See this as a time for cleansing and renewal, a time to find your own rhythm and unleash the human spirit within you. This is a wonderful exercise to do if you are feeling depressed or disconnected from your family, your ancestry, your community, or from spirit. Our bodies are made of water, so water is an ideal medium for self-acceptance, and, *mumoh,* or spirit, is also sound. Through water and sound, you will be transported as an embryo in the womb, and will emerge renewed and transformed. Enjoy!

Continuing on the Sacred Path

As you journey to discover your own rhythm, your own way to spirit, be open-minded and understand that time is not of the essence on this sacred path. It is not like a drive-through fast-food joint where getting served quickly is the whole point. Rather, it is more like a carefully prepared feast to be shared among loving friends. It is up to you to decide how much time you need. Be patient and persistent in knowing that you are perhaps only a moment away from your goal.

The question many ask me is: How do I know when I am there? When that day and time arrives, you will be the first person to notice the change! It is palpable. It is like the sun, bright and beautiful like a rose. Your performance and your experience are enhanced in all areas once your *mishe* essence is activated. You will find that a deep secret and amazing mystery is revealed to you, which will serve as an indicator of a total alignment of body, mind, and spirit. If you are still not sure, make note if your friends are starting to ask questions about your newly acquired air of presence.

To know who you really are in this life, the real question is: What kind of dance do you want to dance? Only by accepting our own true relation with the universe, our own true rhythm, can we, like those dinosaurs who left their footprints at Dinosaur Ridge in Colorado so many millions of years ago, also leave our stories in the sands of times for future generations.

I once was invited to attend a lecture given by Steve Young and friends at the Mormon Church here in Oakland. We had been given VIP tickets, so we were seated in the VIP section at the front of the auditorium. Soon after we had settled into our seats, I started to notice that a middle-aged Caucasian man was staring intently at me. I briefly met his gaze to investigate if perhaps our paths had crossed. There was no sign of any past encounter. Therefore, I returned my attention to the stage, where the program would soon be starting.

Suddenly, out of the corner of my right eye, I saw this man rising and starting to walk toward me. Moments later, I heard a voice saying, "Good evening, my name is John Doe. I am nobody. Who are you?"

I was surprised and embarrassed and wondered if this man was aware of what he was saying! Did he even realize that we were *all* sitting in the VIP section of the auditorium? As the man stretched his hand out for me to shake, I grabbed it and looked deep into his blue eyes. I was awestruck and at a loss over what to say. It was as if we both stood caught for a moment in eternity. Finally I told him my name and introduced him to my wife, Aeeshah. He thanked me and walked back to his seat.

The point of this story is that my new friend's "I am nobody" statement suggested that he did not believe that he was also a "Very Important Person." When we are truly aware of who we are, such mistakes are rare!

In the end, finding our own rhythm and path to spirit, and thus unleashing our spirit, means that our authentic power of choice will be awakened, inevitably opening the doors of infinite possibility. It is my hope that if and when this miracle unfolds for you, you will muster the courage and commitment to share this ocean of peace and love with your beloved community, and allow your community to share the same with you. This is the ultimate circular energy field created by the path of mindful drumming meditation: giving and receiving within a circle of endless love and devotion.

Take the next couple of pages to write notes of your experience or draw pictures.

NOTES

Conclusion

*If we choose the path
of love and peace,
mindful drumming can take us there.
Mindful drumming taps instantly into
humanity's desire for peace,
and actualizes it by harnessing
the vibrations and rhythms of the soul.*

~ Kokomon Clottey

The twin concepts of mindful drumming, rhythm and sound, are indeed catalytic in unleashing the human spirit. As you have discovered, rhythm and sound have always offered important connections in every culture—of human being to Nyogboh, of human being to the ancestral spirits, of human being to nature, and of human being to human being. As you have engaged in the practices in this book, you have journeyed across the valleys and up the mountains to the portals of rhythm and vibration. In doing so, you have been uncovering your own sacred story. I hope that you have been able to drum alone or with a circle of friends while playing simple, fun rhythms, and I hope that this book has aroused your interest in uncovering the mysteries of your being and inspired you to continue to unfold your sacred story through the drum. Whenever you drum, you tap into the essence of the rhythm of life's mysteries.

Mindful drumming offers essential wisdom for today's world. As our population increases, so does competition for limited resources. Our greatest challenges, including war, AIDS, poverty, environmental degradation, and hunger, all have their roots in fear. A deep sense of mistrust in our neighbors inevitably erodes our capacity to create and sustain community. I hope you've had an experience of how the twin concepts of rhythm and sound can serve as powerful media and medicine to remove the blocks to our peaceful coexistence. The drum, sounding the heartbeat of humanity as generated in mindful drumming circles, creates a powerful communal energy that we can utilize for social change and planetary healing.

As we enter the twenty-first century, we are standing at the crossroads of change. Will we continue down the road of attack and defense, or will we dedicate ourselves fully to the great gifts of love and peace? What is it in us that causes us to forget natural healing methods? Why do we choose conflict over peace? Why do we find it so hard to forgive even though we are aware of inevitable personal pain caused by holding on to resentments? How is it that we refuse to learn from our collective history, even though we know that we are condemning ourselves to repeat the same old suffering? What is it in us that causes us to be ignorant and complacent?

Can we imagine a world where no child ever lives in fear? Can we imagine a world where no child is homeless? Can we imagine a world where no child is ever hungry? What would happen if all the world leaders were to drum together in unison?

If we choose the path of love and peace, mindful drumming can take us there. Mindful drumming taps instantly into humanity's desire for peace, and actualizes it by harnessing the vibrations and rhythms of the soul. Mindful drumming as a meditation process does not require years of training for us to develop mastery. In just an hour of creating equal measurements of rhythms, vibrations, and sounds, anyone can be taken into an elevated state of awareness: a trancelike, hypnotic state of awareness in which time stops and everything is immersed in an ocean of love.

Ultimately, mindful drumming can only be experienced. I am leaving you with all the guidance I can share about this path. Do with it as you will. I am releasing the timeless indigenous wisdom of the Ga tribe into your hands! I feel confident that you will know exactly what to do with it. As I said in the Preface, it is no accident that you found this book. As you connect with your personal internal rhythms and sounds, you will tap into an infinite reservoir of joy and peace. Mindful drumming is life-giving. Can you imagine being able to touch your true being—your authentic, free, and deeply happy spirit—at any moment, no matter what state you're in? Mindful drumming provides you with immediate access to *mishe*, a state of being completely blissed out and perfectly happy.

Once again, take a moment and put your hand on your heart and listen. Listen deeply to your heartbeat. This is a sacred rhythm that has been with you always. Heed it. Listen to it. Be it, and unleash it to be free.

The timeless wisdom of indigenous peoples is readily available to us through the eternal resources of rhythm and sound. If we listen to their knowing and put their wisdom into practice through mindful drumming meditation, it is inevitable that we will unleash the tremendous power of our human spirit. For the sake of our very survival, we need to recognize that there is another way—that is, to embrace the practice of community building through mindful drumming, and forge a new relationship with one another as well as a wiser stewardship of Mother Earth.

Wishing you many blessings,

Kokomon Clottey

Appendix A

Glossary

adopeh leprechauns
Agoo! Knock! Hello!
akpeteshie a local Ga drink made from sugarcane or palm wine
Akwaba! Welcome!
Atta-Naa-Nyogboh Father-Mother-God
bosumfo healer
deep listening paying attention with your heart and your whole being
fron-ton-fron a huge ceremonial drum
Hedzoleh! Peace!
Hedzoleh aha bo! Peace be with you!
Hiao! (pronounced *he-ah-oh*) Let it be so! Let it manifest!
Humowoh Hunger tomorrow, hooting at hunger (a Ga festival)
Koryor Wind
kputua a cup made out of a dry coconut shell
libation the process of pouring sacred water or liquid on the Earth as an invocation
mindful drumming Drumming diverse polyrhythms with full attention and presence. Mindful drumming comes from the twin concepts of rhythm and sound. Through the power of mindful drumming meditation, one can attain true joy and happiness. Mindful drumming creates a rhythmic space that brings individuals together collectively to journey to a higher or altered state of consciousness.
mishe happiness
mishe ke sumo happiness and love
Mi sumo bo! I love you!
mumoh spirit; breath

nadi shodhana purification of the channels (an exercise from the *pranayama* tradition that purifies the *nadis* (channels) along which *prana* (life force) flows

Nyogboh Great Spirit; God; the cosmic creative force

Oyiwaladon! (pronounced *o-yee-wah-lah-don*) May eternal blessing and grace be bestowed upon you! Thank you!

prana life energy

pranayama regulation or control of *prana* (life force); breath control

shaman a medicine man or woman with occult knowledge or possessing indigenous spiritual wisdom; a mystic

sumo love

Sumo gbomotso! Love my body!

taakotsa (pronounced *ta-ko-cha*) a local root chewed by the Ga people; chewing sponge

tempo speed

trance an altered state of consciousness, a condition that can evoke *mishe*, or happiness, and is facilitated by mindful drumming meditation

tsofa-tse (pronounced *cho- fa-cheh*) fetish priest or priestess; a shaman or elder among the Ga people

Tswa, tswa, omanye aba! May prosperity be bestowed upon us! May all our wishes be honored and brought to fruition! Blessing be ours no matter the strife!

waku family

Appendix B

Where to Get a Drum, Kinds of Drums and their Origins

Obtaining an African Drum

In the San Francisco Bay Area

SANKOFA
3278 West Street, Oakland, CA 94608
510-652-5530

Berkeley Flea Market
Berkeley BART Station
3100 Adeline (at Ashby), Berkeley, CA
(weekends only)

The Silver Bush World Music Store
Attn.: Amber Godden
42 E. Bolins Rd., Fairfax, CA 94930
415-457-0814

Elsewhere in the United States

Djembe Drums
4628 SW 10th Avenue, Cape Coral, FL 33914
877-803-8633
www.GOATSKINS.com

Motherland Music
5797West Washington Blvd., Culver City, CA 90232
323-965-9839
www.motherlandrhythmart.com

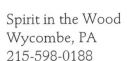

Spirit in the Wood
Wycombe, PA
215-598-0188

Obtaining Other Kinds of Drums

All One Tribe Foundation
P.O. Drawer N, Taos, NM 87571
505-751-0019

Jamtown
P.O. Box 31514, Seattle, WA 98103-1514
206-632-9136

Noisy Toys
Los Angeles, CA
800-874-8223

San Francisco Taiko Dojo
1581 Webster St., Suite 200, San Francisco, CA 94115
415-928-2456
www.taikodojo.org

Tachini Drums
P.O. Box 574, Arlee, MT 59821
www.drumhoops.com

Taos Drums
800-424-DRUM
Fax: 505-758-9844
www.taosdrums.com

Kinds of Drums
and their Origins

Djembe
West African

Doha Drum
Middle East
&
Taiko
Japanese

Fontonfron
West African

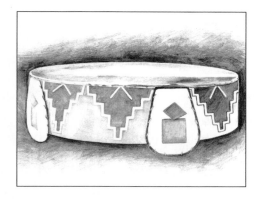

Native American

Tabla
Indian

Surdo
Brazilian Drum

Atumpan (Talk-
ing Drums)
West Africa

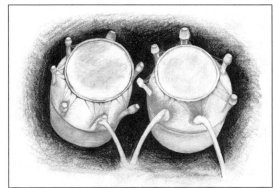

Appendix C

Rhythmic Transcriptions

Musical Notation of the Rhythms

To provide those with musical training with a clearer picture of the rhythms used in mindful drumming, and to point to their source in traditional African rhythms, I sought someone who could transcribe the rhythms and render them as musical notations. You may follow these transcriptions to gain a deeper experience of both traditional African rhythms and some of the mindful drumming rhythms I employ in leading mindful drumming meditations.

In my search to find a transcriber, I contacted Professor C. K. Ladzekpo at the University of California at Berkeley, who introduced me to Matthew Hill. Mr. Hill generously agreed to analyze and transcribe a number of such rhythms. His words are followed by transcriptions of seven traditional African rhythms and seven mindful drumming rhythms.

Traditional and Mindful Rhythms:
Matthew Hill's Comments and Transcriptions

During my time with Kokomon, I spoke with him about drumming in Africa and America, about feeling and moving with music, and about trance. Kokomon stressed the importance of repeating a rhythmic phrase over and over, and he insisted that everyone had to *experience* the healing power of rhythm and vibration, which means not just listening, but playing!

These transcriptions are an attempt to capture some of the essence of Kokomon's drumming. The note values should be played fairly strictly, since they are written to reflect the *swing* inherent in this music. Notes and rests indicate the sequence of percussive strokes. These strokes are allowed to decay naturally, without any dampening. Thus, some drums will ring longer than others. Ties have been avoided.

These examples are mostly "pure rhythm," without any specified pitch. Use high or low pitches, as you like. In a few examples, Kokomon contrasted low-pitched center strokes with higher-pitched rim strokes. The sound of his drum, the nature of his technique, and his rhythmic philosophy do not require the use of a traditional staff.

In African music, it is traditional to keep track of the beat using some type of body movement. But African drumming does not use the same Western concept of *meter*. To play Kokomon's examples, strike every note with equal force and volume. Do not give extra musical weight to the "one" or to on-beat phrases versus syncopated ones.

Traditional African Rhythms

This first rhythm is a two-bar phrase. You can play it all on a single pitch, or alternate, as Kokomon has done.

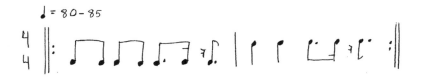

The second rhythm contains some interesting subtleties. As I tried to learn it, Kokomon sang a companion pattern, and this gave me a point of reference. I have written the companion groove below the main one.

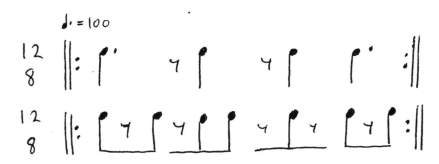

The third rhythm has a funky, off-beat feel. At first, it might be hard to keep feeling the beat without getting turned around. But this is normal.

The fourth rhythm is very profound. When first getting to know the pattern, you may want to think of a call and response between two bars of 6/8. After a while, you should be able to hear the entire pattern as 12/8. It is written both ways.

The fifth rhythm is an old West African pattern. Kokomon called it "the great granddaddy" of many salsa and calypso grooves.

The sixth rhythm comes from northern Ghana. It has fascinating cross rhythms. The first three beats imply dotted sixteenths crossing the main beat. Yet the full phrase remains grounded as a slow and graceful 4/4.

The seventh rhythm is related to the West African *kplanlogo* pattern from number five. Notice how the rhythmic contrast is maintained.

Mindful Drumming Rhythms

The first mindful drumming rhythm is "the heartbeat."

The second mindful drumming rhythm was demonstrated using two pitches, but Kokomon told me that one would be fine also.

The third mindful drumming rhythm is two bars long.

The fourth mindful drumming rhythm uses a rim stroke to contrast with the center strokes.

The fifth mindful drumming rhythm is as follows.

The sixth mindful drumming rhythm can be conceived or written two different ways.

The seventh mindful drumming rhythm used some new techniques. The "x" noteheads indicate gentle grace note touches. Alternate hands right to left. On the fourth beat, strike a flam using both hands.

Appendix D

Other Resources

Workshops on Mindful Drumming

For information about the Attitudinal Healing Connection in Oakland, California, and its workshops, or about the lectures and workshops of Kokomon and Aeeshah Clottey, please contact:

The Attitudinal Healing Connection, Inc. (AHC)
3278 West Street, Oakland, CA 94608
Phone: 510-652-5530   www.ahc-oakland.org
Kokomon and Aeeshah's workshops and retreats are grounded in indigenous wisdom and the principles of attitudinal healing. The AHC also offers continuing education credits to marriage and family therapists (MFTs) and licensed clinical social workers (LCSWs).

Books of Interest

Alternative Medicine. Puyallup, WA: Future Medicine, 1994.

The Adinkra Dictonary: A Visual Primer on the Language of Adinkra. W. Bruce Willis, Washington, D.C., The Pyramid Complex, 1998.

Breath was the First Drummer: A Treatise on Drums Drumming and Drummers. Dru Kristel, Santa Fe, NM, QX Publications/A.D.A.M. Inc., 1995.

Conversations with Ogotemmeli. Marcel Griaule. London: Oxford University Press, 1965.

Drum Circle Spirit: Facilitating Human Potential Through Rhythm. Arthur Hull, Reno, NV, White Cliffs Media, 1998.

Drum Circle: A Guide to World Percussion. Chalo Eduardo & Frank Kummor, Van Nuys, CA, Alfred Publishing Co., Inc. 2001.

Drum Gahu: The Rhythms of West African Drumming. David Locke, Crown Point, IN, White Cliffs Media Company, 1987.

The Drummer's Path: Moving the Spirit and Traditional Drumming. Sule Greg Wilson, Rochester, Vermont, Destiny Books, 1992

Drumming at the Edge of Magic. Mickey Hart with Jay Stevens. New York: HarperCollins, 1990.

Drumming the Spirit to Life, Russell Buddy Helm, St. Paul, Minnesota, Llewellyn Publications, 2000.

Handbook on Drug Abuse Prevention: A Comprehensive Strategy to Prevent the Abuse of Alcohol and Other Drugs. Coombs, R.H. & Ziedonis, D.M. (eds). Boston: Allyn & Bacon, 1995.

The Healing Drum. Yaya Diallo and Mitchell Hall. Rochester, VT: Destiny Books, 1989.

The Healing Power of the Drum, Robert Lawrence Friedman, Reno, NV, White Cliffs Media, 2000

The Healing Wisdom of Africa. Malidoma Patrice Somé. New York:Putman, 1998.

How to Play Djembe: West African Rhythms for Beginners. Alan Dworsky & Betsy Sansby, Minnetonka, MN, Dancing Hands Music, 2000.

Let Your Voice Be Heard: Songs from Ghana and Zimbabwe. Abraham Kobena & Adzinyah & Dumisani Maraire, Judith Cook Tucker, Danbury, CT, World Music Press, 1969.

A Life for the Djembe: Traditional Rhythms of the Malinke. Mamady Keita, Brussel, Belgien: Arun, 1999.

Love Is Letting Go of Fear. Gerald G. Jampolsky. New York: Bantam, 1981.

One River, Many Wells. Matthew Fox. New York: Penguin Putman, 2000.

Original Blessing. Matthew Fox. Santa Fe, NM: Bear & Co., 1983.

Planet Drum. Mickey Hart and Fredric Lieberman. Petaluma, CA: Grateful Dead Books, 1991.

Rhythms and Songs from Guinea, Famoudou Konate & Thomas, Olderhausen, Germany, Lugert Verlag, 2000.

Spirit into Sound: The Magic of Music. Mickey Hart and Fredric Lieberman, Petaluma, CA, Grateful Dead Books, 1999.

Sounds of Healing. Mitchell L. Gaynor, M.D. New York, NY, Broadway Books, 1999.

The Way of the Drum, Russell Buddy Helm, St. Paul, Minnesota, Llewellyn Publications, 2001

Welcoming Spirit Home. Sonbonfu E. Somé. Novato, CA: New World Library, 1999.

Wisdom Circles: A Guide to self-discovery and Community Building in Small Groups. Charles Garfield, Cindy Spring and Sedonia Cahill, New York, Hyperion, 1998.

When the Drummers were Women: A spiritual History of Rhythm. Layne Redmond, New York, Three Rivers Press, 1997.

Organizations of Interest

African Music and Dance Ensemble
C. K. Ladzekpo, Director
1539 6th Avenue, Oakland, CA 94606
510-763-1792
www.cnmat.berkeley.edu/~ladzekpo/Ensemble.htm
Offers workshops and performances from Ghana, West Africa.

Ancestors Wisdom Spring
P.O. Box 4918, Oakland, CA 94605
www.PrimaSounds.com/echoes/
Offers seminars and workshops on indigenous wisdom of the Dagara people, Burkina Faso, West Africa.

ArtEsteem
Attitudinal Healing Connection, Inc.
3278 West Street, Oakland, CA 94608
510-652-5530
artesteem@aol.com
ArtEsteem is the children's after-school program of the Attitudinal Healing Connection, Inc. ArtEsteem was developed in 1995 by Amana Harris, who holds a Bachelor of Fine Arts degree from the California College of Arts and Crafts and a Master's degree in Art and Social Justice from the University of San Francisco. As a teacher in the Oakland Public School District, Ms. Harris saw a deep void in the learning curriculum, combined with poverty and violence in the home and community. She saw this void as an impediment to the children's ability to achieve academic excellence and emotional well-being. She believed that for the children to succeed, they needed art and other learning aids and mentoring to help them see themselves in a positive light. ArtEsteem is a childhood violence prevention program that uses self-reflective art, attitudinal healing principles to increase spiritual awareness, and community-building skills as means to raise self-esteem.

EarthSave
http://www.earthsave.org/
EarthSave leads a global movement of people from all walks of life who are taking concrete steps to promote healthy and life-sustaining food choices.

Greenpeace
www.greenpeace.org
Environmental advocacy group.

Inner Peace Music
P.O. Box 2644, San Anselmo, CA 94979
www.innerpeacemusic.com
Offers music that invokes and inspires the human spirit.

Naropa-University of Creation Spirituality
510-835-4827
www.creationspirituality.com
Offers a Master's degree and a Doctor of Ministry in creation spirituality.

Network for Attitudinal Healing International
33 Buchanan Drive, Sausalito, CA 94965
415-331-4545
Offers workshops and support groups for individuals interested in removing fear and embracing love.

Tribe of Heart
P.O. Box 149, Ithaca, NY 14851
607-275-0806
www.tribeofheart.org
Makes use of storytelling and visual media to present a vision of a compassionate future.

YES!
420 Bronco Road, Soquel, CA 75073
www.yesworld.org
Utilizes poetry, storytelling, and music at summer camps to educate and inspire youth ages fifteen to thirty to be stewards of planet Earth.

About the Author, Contributor, and Editor

Author: Kokomon Clottey

Kokomon Clottey was born to the Ga-Adagbe tribe in Accra, the capital of Ghana in West Africa. The Ga society is rich with ancient codes of conduct, deep spiritual beliefs, and awesome rituals of power. Kokomon is a medicine man and interpreter of this ancient African tribe's wisdom and rituals. It was the local master of the drummers of the Ga tribe who gave him the foundation for his drumming skills.

Kokomon moved to the United States in 1977. He brings to the stage thirty years of performing experience and musical training from the Royal Schools of Music Workshop in London as well as the Dick Grove School of Music.

Kokomon is a many-faceted man capable of painting rainbows in the sky. He is a storyteller, record producer, author, and teacher. He composed and produced the *Gifts of God* audiocassette. Kokomon has also produced two compact disks, *Love Is the Answer,* and *Mystic* Vision, and is the coauthor with his wife Aeeshah of *Beyond Fear: Twelve Spiritual Keys to Racial Healing* (Tiburon, CA: H J Kramer, 1998). He contributed to *Imagine What America Could Be in the Twenty-First Century: Visions of a Better Future from Leading American Thinkers* (Emmaus, PA: Rodale, 2000) and is the author of *Mindful Drumming; Ancient Wisdom for Unleashing the Human Spirit and for Building Community* (2003).

Kokomon is the cofounder of the Attitudinal Healing Connection (AHC), Inc., in Oakland, California, an organization that is internationally recognized for its work in racial healing. The AHC also offers ArtEsteem, a children's after-school program developed by Amana Harris (see Appendix D for more information about this important violence-prevention program that helps youth develop greater self-esteem). Kokomon is also cofounder of the Center for Attitudinal Healing in Ghana, West Africa.

Kokomon can be contacted at the Attitudinal Healing Connection, Inc., 3278 West Street, Oakland, CA 94608; 510-652-5530; healco@aol.com.

Contributor: Dennis "Den" Hill, M.D.

Dennis "Den" Hill was born and raised in the Pacific Northwest, the eldest of five children. He attended the University of Oregon Medical School, where he obtained his M.D. degree, then completed his residency training at the University of California at San Francisco. He practiced medicine in San Francisco for twenty-four years as a cancer physician. He noticed over those years that many of his patients with life-threatening illness showed a deep human dignity that was in contrast with that of the ordinary person. Despite their illness, they seemed to have a healthier, even happier, perspective on life. They were in touch with their human spirit.

Den has been a practicing Buddhist for over fourteen years, and does a mindful chanting practice twice a day to be in rhythm with his own human spirit, or Buddha nature. This firsthand experience with the inner realm of life, along with encouragement from his mentor, Daisaku Ikeda, led him to seek out knowledge of the primordial ways of community which continue to this day in traditional indigenous cultures. These nature-based village cultures honor each individual's spirit as an integral part of their collective community. Den has studied with a variety of teachers over the years, including Malidoma and Sobonfu Somé of the Dagara tribe, and Kokomon Clottey of the Ga people of Ghana, West Africa.

Den is currently a grandfather and an elder in an intentional community of former students of a year-long workshop who continue to gather on a monthly basis. They call themselves, simply, "the village." His interest is helping "modern" people become healthier and happier, and he has spoken publicly on the power of healthy habits and the power of community, based on the timeless wisdom of indigenous cultures.

He lives in Oakland, California, and can be contacted by phone at 510-451-6310 or by e-mail at denhill@mindspring.com.

Editor: Nancy Grimley Carleton

Nancy Grimley Carleton is an editor with over twenty years of experience helping authors and publishers create quality books. She has edited everything from academic texts on psychology and religion to best-selling fiction and self-help books by well-known authors, including Dan Millman, Lynn Andrews, John Robbins, and Sanaya Roman.

She has a B.A. in Humanities from the University of California at Berkeley, where she was a Regents Scholar and graduated Phi Beta Kappa with highest honors, and an M.A. in Transpersonal Counseling Psychology from John F. Kennedy University. She is a licensed psychotherapist (MFT #28313) and maintains a small private practice in addition to working as an editor and consultant.

Nancy brings to her work a dedication to peace, social justice, and spiritual transformation as well as intuitive insight and a firm commitment to helping authors find their own voices. She has been an activist since she was a teenager, and was recognized by the Commission on the Status of Women as an Outstanding Woman of Berkeley in the year 2000. She has served as Chair of Berkeley's Zoning Adjustments Board and as Vice Chair of its Parks and Recreation Commission, as well as on the Boards of a number of nonprofits. One of her proudest achievements has been helping to bring her neighbors together to design, build, plant, and sustain a small community park, Halcyon Commons, where there was once a parking lot.

She lives in Berkeley, California, with her dogs, rabbits, birds, and a hamster, and can be contacted by phone at 510-644-0172 or by e-mail at ngc2@mindspring.com.

Index

Contact Information

Please write and share your experience with mindful drumming; beause, I am writing a book about recovery.

You can obtain information about arranging workshops on mindful drumming in your area, or find out more about the Attitudinal Healing Connection, Inc., by contacting the author:

Kokomon Clottey
Attitudinal Healing Connection, Inc.
3278 West Street
Oakland, CA 94608
kokomon@AHC-Oakland.org
510-652-5530